EDGAR'S MISSION
a farm sanctuary | our mission is kindness

Edgar's Mission is a not-for-profit farm sanctuary with a vision for a humane and just world for all.

The sanctuary is set on 153 peaceable acres near Lancefield, about 60 kilometres north of Melbourne, Australia. Edgar's Mission rescues and provides a safe haven for animals in need, providing lifelong love and care to over 450 rescued animals. Through education, outreach, advocacy, community enrichment and farm tours, the sanctuary encourages people to expand their circle of compassion to include all animals.

Pam Ahern is the founder and director of Edgar's Mission and dedicates her life to the protection of farmed animals. She is the Australian World Animal Day Ambassador. Since 2003, when Pam rescued a piglet and named him Edgar Alan Pig, thousands of farmed animals have been given a second chance at life after making their way through the gates of the sanctuary.

edgarsmission.org.au

Kindness Community

VEGAN COOKBOOK

Food photography by Julie Renouf

Sanctuary photography by Kyle Behrend & Kelly Dinham

Affirm press

'If *we* could live
healthy and happy lives
without harming others,
why wouldn't we?'

EDGAR'S MISSION

Contents

our mission

HEY EWE!

Dear Reader

You've found us! We trust you will come to understand what an important difference this book will make to our lives.

People are often surprised to learn how unique each one of us is. No blanket term can describe us, but 'special' comes close. Very few people stop to think about what our lives are really like – we're rarely seen in our complete and glorious forms. We'd like to change that and share with you a small glimpse of who we really are.

See that photo opposite? There's Polly Pig, she loves to dig, and has a wicked sense of fun. We love it when Pam calls her, and Polly lifts her head in acknowledgement then walks in the opposite direction. Chances are she is off for a wallow in the mud, because pigs, funnily enough, are no good at sweating. Mud cools Polly down.

Oh, and that very handsome rooster? That's Red Baron. When he's not riding around on Pam's shoulder, he is crowing at the office door for a snack. Naturally his human friends oblige. That cute little two-tone pony is Monty – don't ever call him 'Shorty'! He thinks he is the grandest stallion in the land, even though he is actually a pint-sized miniature.

Little Pottsy Lamb just loves scratches under the chin and will even offer a hoof shake. Sound familiar? Last but not least is Julia, a sweet little kid goat who can climb any mountain, even your car!

So, no buts about it, next time you think of talking to us, please just watch us for a bit. See how much we love and cherish our lives and how we will choose joy at every opportunity and go to great lengths to avoid pain. We think it best, too, if you also listen long and hard, not just with your ears, but also with your heart.

With love,

Monty, Joy, Pottsy, Red Baron and Polly

OTWAY

IT TAKES A COMMUNITY OF KINDNESS . . .

Pam Ahern

Founder and director, Edgar's Mission Farm Sanctuary

A far, far younger version of myself sat transfixed watching a movie called *Doctor Dolittle*. Rex Harrison, playing the role of the good doctor, belted out 'Talk to the Animals' – such a catchy song it went on to win an Academy Award. I was captivated by the notion of what fun it would be to 'chat in chimpanzee'. However, over the years, I have been drawn to a grander idea that fosters a more respectful and compassionate view of animals. It's an idea inspired by A. A. Milne, of Winnie-the-Pooh fame: 'Some people talk to animals. Not many listen though. That's the problem.'

And indeed, it is a great problem for my farmed animal friends.

If you had eavesdropped on one of my many joyous mealtimes with Edgar's Mission's eponymous Edgar Alan Pig, you would have heard snippets like these: 'apple', 'peach', 'carrot', 'cucumber – okay, no cucumber', 'grapes – okay, okay, more grapes', 'doughnut', 'little bit more carrot', 'ah, watermelon!'

You will find no finer connoisseur of food than Edgar Alan Pig – he took the greatest of pleasure with each bite and savoured all (bar the cucumber) like it was part of the most delicious meal on the planet. Which it was, after all, having been prepared with all my love and my most basic culinary skills. Yep, you guessed it, I am not the greatest of cooks, but according to dear Edgar I was, and that was all that mattered to me. Oh, how I loved that pig, and the many meals we shared together stand among my greatest memories.

I think you'll agree that few joys in life rival the pleasures garnered from mealtimes with family and friends. Exchanging banter and breaking bread across the table gives the basic necessity of eating food a far, far greater meaning. Since the most ancient of times, people have come together over

food; it is a tradition that transcends cultures and crosses borders the world over. From our ancestors recognising the many benefits of working cooperatively together to bring food to the table, to our modern-day celebrations of birthdays, weddings, sporting achievements and who-needs-an-excuse gatherings, there are few activities that connect us more to the earth, each other and kindness.

There is something so special about food made with the ingredients of love, laughter, family and friends, all prepared in the family home.

When I think back to how this book came into being, I am reminded of the old African proverb, 'It takes a village to raise a child'. An entire community enables a child to grow and experience the world and all of her magic. This book, just like that child, has been nurtured and indeed has flourished courtesy of the extended Kindness Community of Edgar's Mission.

Our sanctuary, firmly planted in the picturesque Macedon Ranges at Lancefield in Victoria, Australia, is like a vast table at which are seated people from across the globe. This table celebrates all that is good in the world:

as its centrepiece, you might find a very handsome rooster named Red Baron, very much alive; in one chair you might find a wee lamb named Rocket Man, cradled in the arms of the kind heart who saved her; you might have to wrestle your chair from an oh-so-lovable dog named Ruby, and share it with a friendly cat named Stitch; and if you listen hard, you might hear not only the sound of a cheeky goat named Tim Tam tapping at the door to come in, but the beating of your heart, reminding you that is the true place for animals to be.

When I first began to share my idea for Edgar's Mission back in 2003, many told me it was a half-baked plan that would never rise – a recipe for disaster, many chimed. But little did they, or I, know of the incredible community who would come together over the years, in so many diverse ways, to make Edgar's Mission steam along as she so amazingly does each awesome and life-changing day. Our community is much like the ingredients of a recipe: they produce something so much greater than the individual ingredients, and all rejoice in knowing of this power. The secret ingredient is the shared belief that a kinder world is not only possible, she is on her way.

She is on her way indeed – from the kitchen, one plant-based meal at a time! Not only will the food nourish your body, the generosity of the community who made it possible will nourish your soul. With each delicious recipe you prepare from the pages of this book, you will be engaging with a community of kindness: a community that listens to the animals and celebrates the bountiful, mouth-watering and cruelty-free world that my beloved Edgar so loved and devoured – a world where we can truly live happy and healthy lives without harming others.

So grab your pots and pans, folks, and let's make a difference!

Pam Ahern

ABOUT *the* RECIPES

The recipes in this book have been collected from all over Australia and New Zealand, and from our global Kindness Community. We asked our supporters for their best recipes, tips and tricks for plant-based eating and were completely blown away by the generosity and shared wisdom.

We selected the recipes so there are options for everyday meals and special occasions, with dishes from many different cultures. These recipes have been tested in the community's kitchens and the methods vary accordingly. Some recipes call for food processors and stand mixers, sometimes they use good old-fashioned elbow grease. One cook's sprinkle is another's carefully weighed portion. We have left any variations in style well alone – far be it from us to mess with a family favourite!

Many of the contributions are from home cooks who've taken a meat-based classic and veganised it, proving you don't have to miss out on anything when living a kinder life. They believe that veganising old favourites is the key to getting the world on board with a kinder way of living, so we've also provided lists of meat and dairy substitutes, as well as information on common ingredients in vegan cooking and amazing hacks. Make sure you check out the Kindness Community Tips that start on page XX – there's a wealth of information based on firsthand experience just waiting for you.

Whether you're a hesitant vegan wondering how you can live without cheese or a veteran vegan baker looking for new ideas, the collective wisdom of the Edgar's Mission Kindness Community has your back.

Spread the message of kindness – get cooking!

SYMBOLS

These symbols will help you decide what recipes to choose:

EASY
no particular skill or equipment required

QUICK
faster than ordering takeaway

MEDIUM
some cooking experience required

WORTH THE EFFORT
best when you have plenty of time

Recipe list

BANANA *and* PEANUT BUTTER MOUSSE

BREAKFAST CASSEROLE

SPICY TOFU SCRAMBLE *with* MUSHROOMS ROCKET *and* AVOCADO

BREAKFAST *of* CHAMPIONS

ANNIE'S UNCANNY PANCAKES

MORGAN'S BREKKY BURRITO

SMOKY MAPLE BAKED BEANS

CHOC RASPBERRY CHIA PUDDING

ACAI BOWL *with* HOMEMADE GRANOLA

BLUENANA BLISS SMOOTHIE BOWL

GRANOLA BARS

FRUITY BREAKFAST BREAD

RISE

& Shine

Start your day
the plant-based way

KYLE BEHREND | COMMUNITY ENGAGEMENT & ADVOCACY, EDGAR'S MISSION

BANANA *and* PEANUT BUTTER MOUSSE

Having worked and volunteered at Edgar's Mission for over 10 years, I don't have to wonder what the animals would say if they could speak. If we asked them what is really important, I think they would say that it is to be kind. I choose to be vegan because their lives matter – to them and to me.

Yes, I eat three bananas almost every day in this mousse. I kind of feel like I'm cheating and eating dessert for breakfast, but it takes 5 minutes to make, fuels me for the day and tastes so good that I haven't switched to anything else.

SERVES 1

- 3 bananas
- 1 tablespoon peanut butter
- 1 tablespoon flaxseed
- 1 tablespoon sunflower seeds
- 1 teaspoon cinnamon
- 1 pear or apple

Peel bananas and place in a bowl. Using a fork, mash the bananas until quite smooth. Mix through the peanut butter, seeds and cinnamon.

Chop the pear or apple into bite-size pieces and add to the banana mixture.

Now you're ready to enjoy your day!

NOTES Swap flaxseeds for chia seeds, and sunflower seeds for pumpkin seeds. ● Swap the apple or pear for other seasonal fruit.

KYM DALY

BREAKFAST CASSEROLE

I adapted a vegetarian recipe I found on Pinterest, which is a great source of inspiration. It is so tasty and satisfying for breakfast, or in fact any meal! I usually serve it with baby spinach leaves and grainy toast.

SERVES 4

- 4–5 medium waxy potatoes, washed
- 40 ml olive oil
- 250 g tempeh, diced into small pieces
- 1 teaspoon smoked paprika
- ¼ cup barbecue sauce
- 1 teaspoon soy sauce
- ½ teaspoon liquid smoke (optional)
- 1 medium onion, chopped
- ½ cup red capsicum, finely diced
- 300 g silken tofu
- 1 tablespoon rice flour or cornflour
- 1 teaspoon turmeric
- 1 teaspoon sweet paprika
- ¼ cup nutritional yeast
- 2 tablespoons chopped shallots
- ¼ teaspoon kala namak (black salt)
- ½ cup vegan cheese, plus extra for sprinkling on top
- chopped chives (optional)
- ½ punnet cherry tomatoes, halved
- pepper

To serve

- baby spinach, toasted grainy bread

Preheat oven to 180°C.

Cut potatoes into small pieces, boil until just soft and put into cold water to stop the cooking process. Set aside.

Heat 15 ml olive oil in a medium frying pan over a medium–high heat and fry the diced tempeh for a few minutes. Lower temperature and add the smoked paprika, barbecue sauce, soy sauce and liquid smoke (if using) and fry for another few minutes. Remove from pan onto a plate, and set aside.

Heat 15 ml olive oil and fry the onion for a few minutes until almost softened. Add the potatoes and capsicum, and fry for 5 minutes or until onion and capsicum are soft and the potatoes have browned a bit.

In a medium bowl combine remaining olive oil, silken tofu, rice (or corn) flour, turmeric, sweet paprika, nutritional yeast, shallots and kala namak. Whisk all these ingredients together, then stir in the vegan cheese and chives (if using).

Add the tempeh and cherry tomatoes to the bowl, season to taste, and mix. Place this mixture into a very lightly greased casserole dish, top with the extra vegan cheese and bake for 30 minutes or until heated through and the cheese is melted and golden.

Serve with baby spinach and toasted grainy bread for a delicious and wholesome breakfast.

NOTES Leftovers will keep in an airtight container in the fridge for up to 3 days. ● Kala namak (black salt) is essential here – that's what gives the 'eggy' smell and flavour. Buy it online from retailers like the Cruelty Free Shop.

LESLEY ECCLES

SPICY TOFU SCRAMBLE *with* MUSHROOMS, ROCKET *and* AVOCADO

A perfect way to start the day, this is my great alternative to scrambled eggs. The combination of spicy, gooey and crunchy makes it a brekky or brunch dish that is super tasty and, better still, good for you!

SERVES 2

- 225 g firm tofu
- 4 portobello mushrooms
- 3 tablespoons olive oil
- ½ red capsicum, julienned
- ¼ teaspoon crushed garlic
- ¼ teaspoon turmeric
- ¼ teaspoon ground cumin
- ¼ teaspoon sriracha (optional)
- good pinch of nutritional yeast (optional)
- salt and cracked black pepper
- 2 slices wholegrain bread

To serve

- 2 cups wild rocket (or any greens)
- 1 avocado, sliced or smashed
- 1 teaspoon black sesame seeds
- coriander leaves
- extra sriracha

Drain or dry tofu with paper towel and place in a bowl, then crumble with a fork.

Brush whole mushrooms with half the oil. Heat a medium-size frying pan, add the mushrooms and cook on medium–high heat till cooked. Set aside but keep warm.

Add remaining oil to the same frying pan, and when hot add the tofu, capsicum, garlic, spices and sriracha (if using). Cook over medium heat mixing well for 5 minutes.

Lastly add the nutritional yeast (if using) to the tofu scramble, season with salt and pepper and cook for a further 5 minutes, stirring occasionally.

While cooking the tofu, start toasting the bread.

Put the toast on warmed plates with the mushrooms to one side, scatter with the rocket and top with the tofu scramble. Add the avocado, black sesame seeds and coriander and serve with extra sriracha on the side.

Bon appétit!

NOTES Leftovers will keep in an airtight container in the fridge for a couple of days. • Kimchi or sauerkraut can be added for a different kind of zing!

CHRIS MAYNE | AFL FOOTBALLER | @CMAYNE23

BREAKFAST of CHAMPIONS

My wife, Britt, and her parents opened my eyes to understand how food gets to our plates, and the changes we need to make for our planet, for animals and for health reasons. I transitioned from vegetarian to vegan around the end of 2016, and I've been lucky to have the support of a great partner and family, and staff at the footy club. Breakfast is the most important meal of the day, and if you ask me, there's nothing better than a bowl of warm rolled oats with all the toppings.

SERVES 1

- 1 cup rolled oats
- 1 cup almond milk (or enough to cover the oats)
- 1 banana
- 3 strawberries or raspberries
- a handful of blueberries
- 2 tablespoons peanut butter
- a sprinkle of puffed quinoa
- a few walnuts, crushed in your hand
- a few dashes of maple syrup

Put the oats and almond milk into a large bowl and cook in the microwave for 2 minutes 30 seconds; otherwise put into a small saucepan on the stove and stir constantly until it's the right texture.

Slice the banana and strawberries or raspberries into bite-size pieces and combine with the blueberries.

When the oats are done, stir through the peanut butter, then top with the fruit, puffed quinoa and walnuts and drizzle with maple syrup.

Take a photo, send it to your family and friends, then stuff your face with goodness!

NOTE Make sure you use a large bowl if you're using the microwave – oats in the microwave tend to overflow!

ANNIE'S UNCANNY PANCAKES

These are best eaten fresh, but on the off-chance there are leftovers, I add them to the kids' school lunchboxes for the next day. I like them with lemon and sugar, and they're also great with berries or jam – whatever takes your fancy. PICTURED ON PAGE 19

MAKES 12 PANCAKES

- 2 cups self-raising flour
- ½ cup caster sugar (adjust as you see fit)
- 1 teaspoon bicarbonate of soda
- 2 teaspoons vanilla extract
- 2 cups plant-based milk (I use soy)
- 3 tablespoons vegan butter (I use Nuttelex), melted, plus extra for pan
- 1 tablespoon white wine vinegar

Combine dry ingredients.

Combine the wet ingredients, and add to the dry ingredients. Mix very well. My tip is to add lightness by whisking in air bubbles. You can also use a blender or Thermomix.

Heat a large non-stick frying pan over medium heat and add a little vegan butter. Pour ¼ cup pancake mixture into the pan and cook for 1–2 minutes or until the edges are set and bubbles appear on the surface. Turn over and cook for a further minute or until cooked through and golden. Repeat with the remaining mixture, adding more vegan butter as you go to make sure pancakes don't stick.

Serve with your favourite topping.

MORGAN'S BREKKY BURRITO

Eating a plant-based diet has helped my recovery after hard workouts and races. My energy levels have increased, and I'm helping the planet and saving animals at the same time. This breakfast burrito is my absolute favourite thing to eat. It's filling, full of protein, and reminds me of my favourite vegan cafe in Phoenix, Arizona – Nami. I use Bio Cheese Cheddar Slices and Vegie Delights brand for the sausages and bacon. **PICTURED ON PAGE 19**

SERVES 1

- 100 g firm tofu
- 2 vegan sausages
- 3 slices vegan bacon
- 1 tablespoon olive oil
- 2 hash browns
- 2 slices vegan cheese
- 1 large tortilla
- hot sauce of your choice (I use Cholula)

To serve

sliced avocado, coriander leaves, lime wedge

Dice the tofu and sausages into 2 cm cubes. Slice or tear the bacon so that it is stringy.

Heat the oil in a frying pan on medium heat. Add tofu to pan and cook until golden brown. Add the hash browns and cook until golden brown.

Add the vegan sausage and cook according to packet instructions.

Heat the tortilla in a microwave or under the grill according to packet instructions, and add the cheese so that it softens and melts.

Once everything in the pan is ready, assemble on the tortilla. Add some sliced avocado, coriander leaves and a squeeze of lime if you wish. Finish with a drizzle of hot sauce all over the filling.

Wrap and enjoy!

NOTES Any filling that doesn't fit in the burrito can be stored in the fridge for lunch the next day. Add brown rice, beans and vegetables of your choice for a great burrito bowl! ● Try making your own Tofu Bacon (see page 215).

FOLLOWING PAGE (clockwise from top left):

Smoky Maple Baked Beans, 20
Morgan's Brekky Burrito
Annie's Uncanny Pancakes, 16
Chocolate Raspberry Chia Puddings, 21

SMOKY MAPLE BAKED BEANS

This baked beans recipe is incredibly easy and far better for you than the tinned variety. Nine ingredients go into a pan and it's really just a matter of warming everything through and serving it up. This is the ultimate recipe for the lazy cook who wants to impress – cafe-style beans at a fraction of the cost! PICTURED ON PAGE 18

SERVES 2

- 1 x 400 g can borlotti beans, drained and rinsed
- 1 x 400 g can butter beans, drained and rinsed
- 1 x 400 g can diced cherry tomatoes
- 1 clove garlic, minced
- 1½ tablespoons smoked paprika
- ¼ teaspoon ground chipotle
- 2 tablespoons maple syrup
- 1 teaspoon vegan Worcestershire sauce
- ½ teaspoon salt, or to taste
- pepper

To serve

sourdough, rocket, sliced avocado

Add all ingredients to a saucepan and cook over a low–medium heat for 5–10 minutes. Taste and adjust seasonings if needed.

Serve with fresh sourdough, lots of peppery rocket, and sliced avocado.

NOTES Leftovers will keep in an airtight container in the fridge for up to 3 days, and can be frozen. ● To intensify the flavours, make the beans a day ahead and heat them up when you're ready. ● If you don't have any ground chipotle, substitute more paprika and some chilli flakes. ● A hash brown on the side is also delicious.

CHOCOLATE RASPBERRY CHIA PUDDINGS

This is an easy breakfast (or snack) that you can whip up the night before, saving those precious minutes in the morning. It will keep you full for a long time. Chia seeds are a great plant-based protein that packs a big nutrient punch – not only are they high in antioxidants, they are a great source of dietary fibre, omega-3 and omega-6 fatty acids, calcium, phosphorus and zinc. PICTURED ON PAGE 18

SERVES 2

- 1 x 400 ml can coconut cream
- 1 cup frozen raspberries
- 2 tablespoons maple syrup
- 2 tablespoons cacao powder
- 1 teaspoon vanilla extract
- 4 tablespoons chia seeds

To serve

- coconut flakes
- fresh raspberries

Place everything except the chia seeds in a blender or food processor and blitz on high until the mixture is smooth.

Add the chia seeds and stir through to combine.

Pour the mixture into serving cups or mason jars and pop in the fridge for at least 2 hours, or overnight, to set.

Serve topped with fresh raspberries and coconut flakes.

NOTES The puddings will keep in the fridge for up to 2 days. • A dollop of Vanilla Bean Cashew Yoghurt (see page 202) would work well with the puddings.

ACAI BOWL *with* HOMEMADE GRANOLA

Eating an acai bowl for breakfast is essentially like waking up and immediately having dessert. But because acai berries are a superfood, you can get away with it. When I was living in the endless summer of LA I was eating a lot of acai bowls. This recipe is an attempt to recreate the creaminess of my favourite one. It's a very simple recipe, but it is the result of some experimentation. Sweet enough, creamy enough, not too icy or runny.

SERVES 2

Acai mix

- ½ cup plant-based milk
- 2 frozen bananas
- ½ cup frozen berries
- 100 g frozen acai

Granola

- 2 cups rolled oats
- ¼ cup almonds, chopped
- ¼ cup sunflower seeds or pepitas
- ½ teaspoon ground cinnamon
- ½ teaspoon ground ginger
- 1 teaspoon sea salt
- ¼ cup maple syrup
- 2 tablespoons olive oil or coconut oil

Toppings

Choose from: granola, sliced banana, sliced strawberries, blueberries, any other fresh fruit of your choice, nut butter, nuts and seeds, coconut yoghurt

FOR THE GRANOLA, preheat oven to 180°C.

Put everything on a non-stick baking tray, mix well to coat the ingredients with syrup and oil, spread evenly over the tray and bake for 15 minutes, then stir. Bake for another 15 minutes. Depending on how big or small your baking tray is, the granola could surprise you and brown very quickly, so keep an eye on it. Take out of the oven and leave to cool.

FOR THE ACAI MIX, put all the ingredients into a food processor, for best results, or a high-speed blender.

The mix requires 3 or 4 minutes of blending. Don't be perturbed if it looks too thick – it's supposed to be thick. Nobody likes a runny acai bowl. If it's so thick that it's not blending, add a splash of plant-based milk.

Pour the acai mix into a bowl and cover with granola and your choice of fruit, nut butter and so on – you pretty much slam it all together.

NOTES This makes enough granola for quite a few acai bowls (depending on how much you snack on it). Stored in an airtight container for about a month. • For a less sweet bowl, replace half a frozen banana with half a frozen zucchini.

BLUENANA BLISS SMOOTHIE BOWL

'Breakfast is the most important meal of the day.' This slogan was part of a clever ad campaign in the 1960s, and still rings true. I find the best way to start any beautiful summer day is with a fruit-rich, sweet and creamy smoothie bowl. Thicker than the average smoothie, this recipe is easy to make, and you can substitute the fruits and seeds with your favourites, or whatever you have on hand.

SERVES 1

- 200 ml soy milk
- 1 frozen banana
- ½–1 cup frozen blueberries (depending how thick and sweet you like your smoothie)
- 1 tablespoon ground linseed
- 1 x serve vanilla vegan protein powder

Toppings

handful of frozen raspberries, cacao nibs, hemp seeds, coconut flakes

Put all the smoothie ingredients into a high-speed blender and process until smooth and creamy.

Pour into a bowl and top with the frozen raspberries, cacao nibs, hemp seeds and coconut flakes.

NOTES It is easier to peel bananas before they're frozen.
• Store peeled bananas in a sealed container in the freezer.

GRANOLA BARS

These granola bars make the perfect on-the-go breakfast or healthy snack at any time of the day. They're super easy to make, and are full of fibre and protein. And not only are they cheaper and healthier than store-bought muesli bars, there are no individual wrappers or artificial additives in sight!

MAKES 12–16 SLICES

- 125 g raw coconut oil
- ½ cup maple syrup or rice syrup
- 1 tablespoon vanilla extract
- ¼ cup plant-based milk of choice
- 2 cups rolled oats
- 1 cup almond meal
- ½ cup hulled hemp seeds, pepitas or sunflower seeds
- 2 tablespoons ground flaxseed or chia
- 1 teaspoon cinnamon
- 2 tablespoons pea protein (optional)
- ½ cup vegan chocolate chips

Preheat oven to 180°C. Line a 20 x 30 cm slice tin with baking paper.

Place the coconut oil, syrup, vanilla and milk in a saucepan. Heat on low until the coconut oil has melted. Mix well and set aside.

In a large bowl, mix the rolled oats, almond meal, hemp seeds, flaxseed, cinnamon and pea protein (if using).

Add the coconut oil mix to the dry ingredients and mix well. Add the chocolate chips and mix well.

Transfer mixture to pan and flatten out evenly to around 2.5 cm thick.

Bake for 20–25 minutes until top is golden.

Remove from the oven and press a spatula over the slice to compress it further – this helps it hold together better once cool. Leave to cool in the tray, then cut into your preferred bar size.

NOTES Store in an airtight container in the fridge for 7–10 days. ● Instead of chocolate chips, use half a block of Loving Earth vegan chocolate, chopped.

MICHAEL THOMAS

FRUITY BREAKFAST BREAD

This delicious and wholesome loaf offers a golden opportunity to show people that heathy food is not necessarily bland, and that choosing non-animal products is easy when making smart dietary choices. The loaf is delicious warm with some plant-based yoghurt and berries, or toasted with peanut butter.

MAKES 1 LOAF

- 3 tablespoons flaxseed meal
- 2 cups plain flour
- ⅔ cup brown sugar
- ⅔ cup dates, chopped
- ½ cup sultanas
- ⅓ cup sunflower seeds
- 1 tablespoon cinnamon
- 1 teaspoon mixed spice
- 1 teaspoon baking powder
- 1 teaspoon bicarbonate of soda
- pinch of nutmeg
- pinch of salt
- ½ cup plant-based milk
- ⅓ cup olive oil
- 2 medium bananas, mashed

Topping

- pecans, chopped
- maple syrup, for drizzling

Preheat oven to 180°C. Grease a medium loaf tin and line with baking paper.

Make a flax egg by combining flaxseed meal and 100 ml warm water in a small bowl and stirring well. Allow to set while you mix the rest of the ingredients.

In a large bowl, combine all remaining loaf ingredients. Add the flax egg then use a wooden spoon to mix all ingredients until a runny consistency forms. If the mixture is too stiff, add more plant-based milk.

Pour mixture into tin. Sprinkle top with pecans and then drizzle with maple syrup.

Bake for 45 minutes or until the top is golden and a skewer inserted into the centre comes out clean. Remove from tin and cool on a rack.

NOTE The loaf will keep in the fridge for a week, either in an airtight container or well wrapped.

'I wake up every day feeling *blessed* that I've made *changes* that will benefit animals *who* deserve life too.'

AMANDA ATTARD

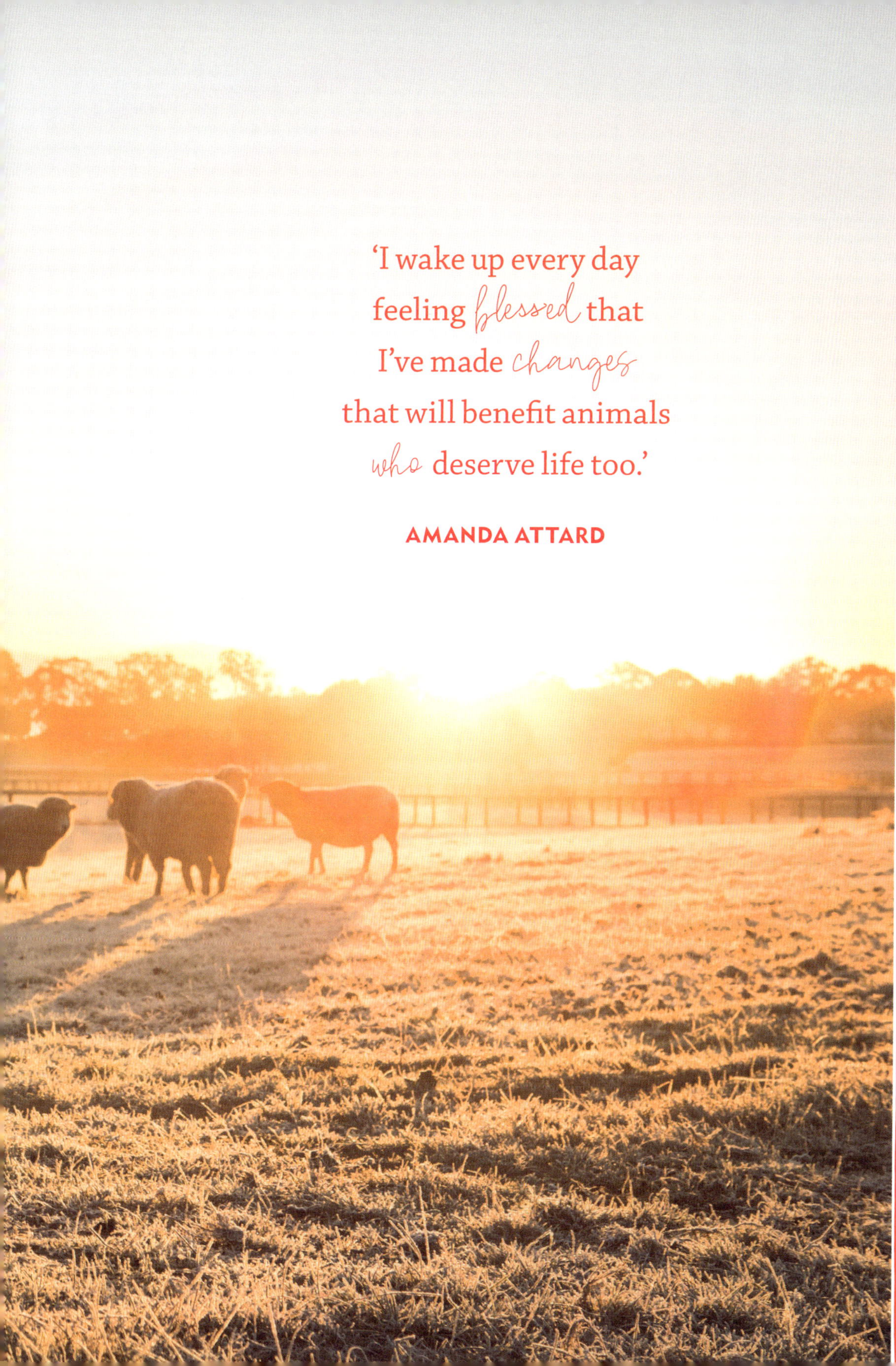

Recipe list

TOFU BOWL *with* PEANUT SAUCE

SWEET *and* SOUR TOFU BALLS

SOUL NOURISH BOWL

POKIE NADDLES

SMOKY TOFU BUDDHA BOWL *with* COCONUT RICE

KHICHARI (SAVOURY DAL *and* RICE)

MIDDLE EASTERN CAULIFLOWER SALAD

PANISSE (FRENCH CHICKPEA FRIES)

GADO GADO

KALE SALAD *with* ROASTED CHICKPEAS

SPICY CREAMY PUMPKIN SOUP

THAI RED CURRY NOODLE SOUP

BEAUTIFUL BEETROOT BORSCHT

VEGAN RAMEN *in* A CREAMY BROTH

HEARTY WARMING MINESTRONE

EASY-PEASY TURMERIC LAKSA *with* TEMPEH

HEART WARMING MINESTRONE

LEEK CHOWDER

A BOWL *of* SUNSHINE

BOWLS *of kindness*

Nourish your soul *with* rice, soups and salads

TOFU BOWL *with* PEANUT SAUCE

You might think going vegan would be limiting, but it's the opposite for me. Rather than just eating the same go-to things, I am constantly researching and trying new things. This is an easy, yummy, healthy weeknight dinner. For speed, buy pre-marinated tofu.

SERVES 2

- 100 g brown basmati rice
- 2 teaspoons sesame oil
- 250 g firm tofu (pre-marinated), cubed
- 200 g broccolini
- handful of green beans, topped and tailed
- bunch of asparagus, trimmed
- two big handfuls of baby spinach, washed
- sesame seeds (optional)

Sauce

- 2 big spoonfuls of peanut butter
- 1 tablespoon soy sauce
- 1 teaspoon finely grated ginger
- squeeze of lime juice
- 2 tablespoons coconut milk
- squeeze of sriracha or other chilli sauce
- 2 teaspoons hoisin sauce (Ayam brand is vegan)
- 2 teaspoons brown sugar

FOR THE SAUCE, mix all the ingredients together in a bowl with the remaining teaspoon of sesame oil. Add a little water to thin the sauce until it's pouring consistency.

TO ASSEMBLE, place a handful of spinach in each bowl, then arrange the rice, vegies and tofu on top. Divide the peanut sauce between the bowls. Sprinkle sesame seeds on top if desired.

NOTES Leftovers will keep in an airtight container in the fridge for 2 days. ● Use this recipe as a starting point, substituting or adding any vegies you fancy. ● Make your own marinade to taste using soy sauce, water, sriracha and brown sugar. Cut firm tofu into cubes, and marinate for at least 30 minutes, or longer to allow the flavours to develop.

SWEET *and* SOUR TOFU BALLS

I learned of this recipe thanks to Robyn Kirby, a good friend of my daughter, Pam. Robyn told me the recipe is originally from *The Tofu Cookbook* by Leah Leneman. I've been making it for over 20 years, and it's always a hit. I was vegetarian and decided to be vegan, alongside Pam, because I was chief chef! I am now a very fit and healthy 82-year-old vegan.

SERVES 4

Tofu balls

250 g firm tofu, sliced
2 tablespoons wholemeal flour
½ teaspoon sea salt
vegetable oil, for frying
brown or white rice, to serve

Sauce

1 tablespoon cornflour
1 x 225 g can pineapple pieces, strained, juice retained
100 ml apple cider vinegar
3 ½ tablespoons raw sugar
3 tablespoons soy sauce
1 medium green capsicum, chopped
2 spring onions, sliced

FOR THE TOFU BALLS, wrap tofu in paper towel and squeeze to remove any liquid. Place in a bowl, mash well, and stir through wholemeal flour and salt. Form into small balls.

Heat the vegetable oil in a frying pan and shallow-fry the tofu balls until golden brown. Drain well on paper towels.

FOR THE SAUCE, dissolve the cornflour in a little pineapple juice and combine with remaining juice, vinegar, sugar and soy sauce in a wok or large saucepan over medium heat. Bring to the boil, then reduce heat, stirring constantly until thickened.

Add tofu balls, capsicum, spring onion and pineapple pieces and heat through.

Serve on a bed of rice. Yummy!

NOTE Leftovers will keep in an airtight container in the fridge for a couple of days, if you're lucky enough to have any!

SOUL NOURISH BOWL

My husband, Alexander, and I absolutely adore cooking nutritious plant-based meals. We love to experiment and play around with new ideas for nutritious plant-based meals. This is one we cooked together, and the result was absolutely delicious! It's now on high rotation.

SERVES 4

- 5 medium white potatoes
- 2 small sweet potatoes
- 1 cup vegetable stock
- salt and pepper
- 1 head broccoli, cut into florets
- 2 medium or 4 small beetroot, peeled and grated
- 2 large or 3 small-to-medium carrots, peeled and grated
- 4 cups spinach, chopped

Coconut rice

- 1 x 400 ml can coconut milk
- 2 cups jasmine rice

Tempeh

- 2 tablespoons coconut aminos
- 1 teaspoon paprika
- ½ teaspoon garlic powder
- 1 x 300 g packet plain tempeh

Tahini sauce

- ½ cup tahini
- ¼ cup lemon juice
- 2 cloves garlic, crushed
- 2 tablespoons nutritional yeast

Preheat oven to 180°C. Line a baking tray with baking paper.

Wash the potatoes and sweet potatoes and cut into bite-size pieces, leaving the skin on.

Pour the vegetable stock into a shallow bowl and dip each piece into the stock before placing it on the tray. Set remaining vegetable stock aside. Season with salt and pepper and place in the oven for 30–45 minutes or until cooked through and golden.

FOR THE COCONUT RICE, place the coconut milk and 1½ cups of water into a saucepan and bring to the boil. Rinse rice, add to the saucepan and simmer for 25–30 minutes until cooked, stirring as required.

FOR THE TEMPEH, in a shallow bowl mix together the coconut aminos, 2 tablespoons of the vegetable stock, paprika, garlic powder and a pinch each of salt and pepper to make a paste.

Slice the tempeh into 8 strips. Using a spoon or brush, cover each slice evenly with the paste. Cook the tempeh in a non-stick pan for 2 minutes on each side until golden, and place to the side.

Bring a small saucepan of water to boil, then simmer broccoli florets for around 5 minutes.

FOR THE SAUCE, mix together the tahini, lemon juice, garlic, nutritional yeast, a pinch of salt and around ½ cup of cold water with a spoon until it's a runny consistency. Add more water if required.

To assemble, divide the coconut rice between 4 bowls, then arrange all other ingredients on top. Put the tahini sauce in a small jug for serving so each person can add their desired amount.

POKIE NADDLES

This take on a poke bowl was created one weeknight when I was trying to pack a lot of goodness and tastiness into one bowl without having to spend hours in the kitchen. The result was delicious, and my partner, Holly, scored it 10/10, so now it's a weekly menu item. It has a bit of everything, and when you put it all together, you go 'YUM!'

SERVES 4

- 4 potatoes
- 1 medium sweet potato
- 12 snow peas, blanched
- ⅓ cup pepitas
- 2 tablespoons black sesame seeds
- 1 tablespoon olive oil
- 100 g mushrooms (I use oyster or baby king)
- 2 tablespoons sake (optional)
- 2 teaspoons brown miso paste
- 600 g sweet potato noodles
- 1 avocado, sliced
- 1 cup shredded red cabbage
- 1 tomato, cubed
- 1 x 200 g packet chilli tofu, sliced
- salt and pepper
- vegan mayonnaise, to serve

Dressing

- ½ cup mentsuyu dressing (see page 212)
- 1 tablespoon rice wine vinegar
- 1 teaspoon sesame oil
- 1 clove garlic, crushed
- 2 cm piece of ginger, grated
- ¼ long red chilli, finely sliced
- ¼ red onion, finely diced

Preheat oven to 180°C. Line an oven tray with baking paper.

FOR THE VEGIES, peel the potatoes and sweet potatoes and chop into small cubes. Place the potato on oven tray, drizzle with olive oil and season. Then roast for 30 minutes, adding the sweet potato after 15 minutes.

In a bowl, blanch the snow peas for 20 seconds in boiling water. Drain and run under cold water.

Heat a frying pan and toast pepitas and sesame seeds. Place in a small bowl.

Using the same frying pan, heat 1 tablespoon olive oil and fry mushrooms until golden brown. Add sake (or water) and miso, and stir until well combined. Reduce liquid a little and remove from heat.

FOR THE NOODLES, cook according to packet instructions, drain and run under cold water. Set aside.

FOR THE DRESSING, whisk all ingredients together.

Divide the noodles between 4 bowls, and arrange all the other ingredients as you like. Spoon dressing over the top, and finish with pepitas and sesame seeds and a dollop of mayo.

NOTES Leftovers will keep in an airtight container in the fridge for up to 3 days. ● I prefer Dutch cream or Sebago potatoes. ● Sweet potato noodles can be found in most Asian grocers. Also check the health food aisle of your supermarket. ● I use Beijing Chilli Tofu, which can be found in most supermarkets.

SMOKY TOFU BUDDHA BOWL *with* COCONUT RICE

This recipe is perfect when you're craving something healthy and satisfying. It might seem like a lot of ingredients, but it will only take about 30 mins to whip up! Get creative with whatever you have at home – tempeh can replace the tofu if you wish. **PICTURED ON PAGE 39**

SERVES 2

Coconut Rice

- 1½ cups rice
- 2 tablespoons coconut milk
- 1 tablespoon desiccated coconut
- a few curry leaves (optional)
- 1 red chilli, sliced (optional)

Marinated tofu

- 220 g firm tofu
- 1 teaspoon liquid smoke
- 1 ½ tablespoons nutritional yeast
- 1 tablespoon tamari
- 1½ tablespoons sesame oil
- pinch of ground chipotle or smoked paprika
- 1 teaspoon rice malt syrup or maple syrup

Vegies

- ¾ cup corn kernels
- 4–6 broccoli florets
- ½ cup edamame
- 2 carrots
- a couple of handfuls of leafy greens
- sesame seeds and hemp seeds (optional)

FOR THE COCONUT RICE, put all the ingredients into a rice cooker, add water according to manufacturer's instructions and cook . While the rice is cooking, prepare the rest of the meal.

FOR THE MARINATED TOFU, cut the tofu into 6 slices, then cut in half lengthways. Mix the remaining ingredients together. Dip each tofu strip in the marinade, then place them in a non-stick pan over medium heat and cook for a few minutes until each side is golden. Once the tofu is cooked, remove from the pan.

FOR THE VEGIES, in the same pan as used for the tofu, cook the corn for about 5 minutes or until cooked through and any leftover marinade has been soaked up.

Steam the broccoli and edamame beans for 5–10 minutes till tender.

Grate the carrot and wash the greens.

TO ASSEMBLE, when the rice is cooked, arrange everything in bowls, top with seeds and dig in!

NOTES Leftovers will keep in an airtight container in the fridge for 3–4 days. • The coconut rice is best made on the day. • If you don't have a rice cooker, see Coconut Rice recipe on page 34. • The tofu can be prepared earlier and left to marinate for several hours. • Save time by using frozen broccoli, edamame and corn.

FOLLOWING PAGE (clockwise from top right):
Smoky Tofu Buddha Bowl with Coconut Rice
Khichari (Savoury Dal and Rice), 40
Middle Eastern Cauliflower Salad, 41

KHICHARI (SAVOURY DAL *and* RICE)

This recipe is from Angela Wiegard, player chef at Collingwood Football Club, and it's one of my favourites – it's delicious. We often have it for lunch a couple of days after a game when we're doing lighter training and need something that is nourishing and good for us. Thanks, Ange! .

PICTURED ON PAGE 39

SERVES 2–4

Dal

- 1 cup basmati rice
- ⅔ cup yellow or red split peas, lentils, mung or toor dal

Spices

- 2 tablespoons oil
- 3 tablespoons ginger, minced or finely chopped
- 1 tablespoon cumin seeds
- 1 tablespoon mustard seeds
- 1 heaped tablespoon ground turmeric (or to taste)
- salt
- sugar (optional – I add a teaspoon)

To serve

- sweet potato, diced and roasted
- plain coconut yoghurt
- fresh coriander leaves
- pickled vegetables (for example, carrots, cabbage, greens, raw beetroot, radishes)

Bring the rice, pulses and 9 cups water to the boil in a large pot. Reduce to a very gentle simmer with a lid on and cook until the dal is tender (at least 1½ hours), stirring often.

You might need to add a little more water as it cooks, especially towards the end of the cooking process as it can easily stick to the bottom of the pot. If your dal does indeed stick, take the pot off the heat and let it sit for a few minutes with the lid on to allow it to steam. Then take the lid off and give it a really good stir.

When it's cooked, the dal should resemble thick porridge.

Heat a non-stick frying pan over medium heat and add the oil. Add the ginger, cumin and mustard seeds and sauté until the seeds 'dance' or pop.

Add to the dal, stir through the turmeric and season with salt to taste. Add a pinch of sugar if you feel it needs it.

Serve with some warm roasted sweet potato, a dollop of plain coconut yoghurt, coriander leaves and pickle.

NOTES Leftovers will keep in an airtight container in the fridge for a couple of days. The dal will get very thick once it's cold. To re-heat, add a little water to the pan and stir over medium heat. ● Dal is traditionally eaten with a salty rather than sweet pickle.

MIDDLE EASTERN CAULIFLOWER SALAD

This delicious and quick-to-make salad is packed with flavour and nutrition. Use whatever dried fruit, herbs and vegetables you have on hand or that are in season. And the best thing is, this versatile salad can be the star of the show, or the support act. PICTURED ON PAGE 38

SERVES 4–6

- ½ – 1 cauliflower
- 1 x 400 g can lentils, drained
- Spanish or spring onion
- herbs of choice (mint, parsley, coriander, chives or dill)
- 5 dried apricots
- handful of sultanas
- 1 fig
- 3 radishes
- 1 capsicum
- 10 almonds
- extra virgin olive oil
- vegan haloumi (I use Hello Friend)
- wedges of roast pumpkin, to serve

Dressing

- 2 tablespoons tahini
- 1–2 lemons, juiced
- 1 teaspoon apple cider vinegar
- 1 tablespoon tamari
- salt and pepper

Coarsely grate the cauliflower into a large serving bowl. Add the lentils to the bowl.

Roughly chop the remaining ingredients (except the haloumi) and add to the bowl.

Cut the haloumi into strips. Heat a little oil in a non-stick pan and cook the haloumi on both sides until golden brown. Drain on paper towel.

Mix all the dressing ingredients and season to taste.

When you're ready to eat, add the dressing to the salad, toss, and top with the haloumi and an extra squeeze of lemon.

Serve with wedges of roast pumpkin.

NOTES Leftover salad (without the dressing) will keep in an airtight container in the fridge for 3 days. • Leave the lentils out, or substitute other beans. • The salad also works well with creamy polenta or beans, and is delicious in a wrap the next day.

CAMILLE RICHARD | @CAMILLE_IN_THE_KITCHEN

PANISSE (FRENCH CHICKPEA FRIES)

I'm a French chef and naturopath, now cooking and running classes in Mansfield, country Victoria. In the South of France, chickpea flour is used a lot to make amazing dishes, both savoury and sweet. Crisp on the outside, creamy on the inside, these are so simple to make, and yet incredibly yummy with just a side salad.

SERVES 8

- 250 g chickpea flour
- ½ teaspoon ground cumin
- salt and pepper
- 80 ml olive oil, plus extra for frying

Put the flour, cumin, salt and pepper in a large saucepan. Gradually whisk in 500 ml water. Over medium heat, keep whisking, and when the mixture is starting to thicken up gradually add up to 500 ml water and the olive oil. Whisk for 10–15 minutes until the mixture is thick and smooth.

Transfer the mixture to a rectangular glass dish. Cover with foil and leave to cool for about 30 minutes before putting in the fridge. When it's completely cold, slice into rectangles or fingers. Leaving it overnight is ideal.

Heat some olive oil in a frying pan over medium–high heat. When the oil is hot, fry the panisse on each side until crispy and golden. Serve immediately.

NOTES Keep the uncooked panisse in an airtight container in the fridge for up to 5 days. Fry when you're ready to eat. ● The uncooked panisse freeze well too – just make sure the mixture is really cold before freezing to avoid crystallisation.

GADO GADO

Gado gado is a great Indonesian salad with peanut sauce. I've shared here what I usually use, but you can use any vegetable you fancy – shredded carrot, sweet potato, cucumber, tomatoes . . . whatever is in season. Look for a variety of leaves as well as colour.

SERVES 2

¼ head of cabbage, sliced

200 g green beans, trimmed and cut into 3 cm lengths

2 potatoes, cut into 2 cm cubes

300 g firm tofu, cut into 1 cm cubes

peanut oil, for frying

handful of mung bean sprouts, tails removed

rice crackers

Peanut sauce

3 shallots

2 cloves garlic

1 thumb-sized piece of young ginger, peeled and roughly chopped

1 tablespoon palm sugar

½ teaspoon white pepper

juice of half a small lemon or lime

3 kaffir lime leaves, torn and woody middle vein removed

1 green or red chilli (optional)

2 handfuls of lightly toasted salted peanuts

Wash and blanch the cabbage and green beans. It's nice to keep a bit of crunch in the greens. Boil or steam the potatoes until tender.

Fry the tofu in some peanut oil until lightly browned.

For the sauce, put all the ingredients in a blender with 100 ml water and blitz. I like the texture to be a bit coarse – using a mortar and pestle will make the texture just right.

Place the vegetables in a bowl, top with sprouts and drizzle with the peanut sauce just before serving. Serve with rice crackers.

NOTES The sauce can be made a day in advance and will keep in a jar in the fridge for up to 3 days. ● If you don't have palm sugar, use brown or white sugar.

CAMILLE RICHARD | @CAMILLE_IN_THE_KITCHEN

KALE SALAD *with* ROASTED CHICKPEAS

When I first served this salad at my vegan cafe, people loved it so much that it became a classic – it's been on the menu for a year now! It's really simple and delicious, and all made from wholefoods ingredients.

PICTURED ON PAGE 47

SERVES 5

- 1 small sweet potato, peeled and diced
- olive oil
- ¼ teaspoon cinnamon
- ½ teaspoon cumin
- salt and pepper
- 1 x 400 g can chickpeas, drained and rinsed
- 1 bunch kale, washed
- 40 g slivered almonds
- 60 g goji berries
- 60 g spinach leaves

Dressing

- ½ cup tahini
- ½ cup olive oil
- 2 tablespoons tamari
- 1 tablespoon lemon juice
- 1 tablespoon maple syrup
- pinch of salt

FOR THE DRESSING, put the tahini in a medium bowl and add the olive oil. Whisk to thin it a bit, then add the rest of the ingredients. Add a little water to reach the desired consistency.

FOR THE SALAD, mix the diced sweet potato with a little olive oil, the cinnamon and half the cumin. Season with salt and pepper. Spread on a tray lined with baking paper and bake in the oven for about 15–20 minutes or until soft. Set aside to cool.

Coat the chickpeas with a little olive oil and the rest of the cumin, and season with salt and pepper. Spread them on another tray lined with baking paper and roast for about 20 minutes, shaking them every now and then. Set aside to cool.

Remove the stems from the kale and chop the leaves, keeping them quite chunky. Put in a bowl with some olive oil, salt and pepper. Massage the kale with your fingers for 2 minutes to break down the fibres.

Add the almonds, goji berries, spinach leaves, chickpeas and sweet potato. Toss with some of the tahini dressing.

SPICY CREAMY PUMPKIN SOUP

Pumpkin soup is one of the first dishes I learnt to cook as a teenager. Over time I took up several recipes and made my own versions. Then when I became vegan I adapted again. It's my go-to comfort food on a cold day – it warms both body and soul. PICTURED ON PAGE 46

SERVES 6–8

- ½ jap pumpkin
- ½ butternut pumpkin
- 5 potatoes
- 2 cups vegetable stock
- 1 brown onion
- 2 sticks celery
- 3 cloves garlic
- 1 red chilli (deseeded if hot)
- olive oil, for frying
- 1 teaspoon ground coriander
- 1 teaspoon ground cumin
- 1 x 400 g can tomatoes
- 1 x 400 g can coconut milk
- fresh coriander, to serve

Peel and chop the pumpkin and potatoes, place in large saucepan with the stock (add extra water if vegetables are not covered with liquid) and simmer until soft.

Finely chop the onions, garlic, celery and chilli, and sauté in olive oil in a saucepan until soft. Add ground coriander and cumin, then tomatoes. Heat through and then remove from heat.

Partially drain the potatoes and pumpkin, keeping roughly 2 cups of stock with the vegetables. (If there's any extra stock, reserve in case you need to thin the soup a little.)

Add the tomato mix along with the coconut cream, and process until smooth with a stick blender or in a traditional blender.

If the soup is too thick, add a little water or stock and blend further. Season with salt and pepper.

Serve hot, topped with fresh coriander.

NOTE The soup will keep in an airtight container in the fridge for up to a week. It also freezes well.

FOLLOWING PAGE (clockwise from top right):

Beautiful Beetroot Borscht, 49
Kale Salad with Roasted Chickpeas, 44
Spicy Creamy Pumpkin Soup
Thai Red Curry Noodle Soup, 48

THAI RED CURRY NOODLE SOUP

This delicious hearty soup is like a warm hug for the soul. Packed full of vegies, noodles, herbs and tofu, it really packs a punch. Mop it up with some crusty bread . . . delicious! We love tofu. It's naturally gluten-free, and an excellent source of protein, iron and calcium. Tofu contains nine essential amino acids, and is full of magnesium, copper, zinc and vitamin B1.

PICTURED ON PAGE 46

SERVES 4–6

- 1 tablespoon olive oil
- 1 brown onion, finely diced
- 1 red capsicum, finely chopped
- 2 cloves garlic, crushed
- 2.5 cm piece of ginger, peeled and grated
- ½ tablespoon curry powder
- ½ teaspoon cumin
- 1 cup pumpkin, peeled and cubed
- 1½ tablespoons red curry paste
- 1 400 ml can coconut milk
- ½ tablespoon tamari (or soy sauce)
- 1 vegie stock cube
- 350 g firm tofu, cubed
- 1 heaped tablespoon nutritional yeast
- chilli flakes, to taste
- 200 g vermicelli rice noodles

To serve

fresh coriander, lime wedges, red onion, chilli

Heat the oil in a large soup pot and add the brown onion. Sweat for 5 minutes, stirring often to avoid burning.

Add the capsicum and soften for 1–2 minutes before adding the garlic, ginger, curry powder and cumin. Cook for a few more minutes until fragrant. Add the pumpkin with a big splash of water, put the lid on and cook for 5 minutes until the pumpkin starts to soften.

Add the curry paste, coconut milk, tamari, crumbled stock cube, tofu, nutritional yeast, chilli flakes (if using), 3 cups boiling water and season to taste. Stir until combined and slowly bring back to the boil.

Once bubbling, add the noodles and reduce heat. Cook for another 5 minutes. If the soup is too thick, add more liquid.

Serve hot, topped with freshly chopped coriander, lime wedges, red onion and chilli, to taste.

NOTES The soup will keep in the fridge for up to 3 days, but note that the noodles will soak up all the soup. • For a milder taste, add less curry paste although this might affect the colour of your soup. • This soup is a great way to use up any vegies.

BEAUTIFUL BEETROOT BORSCHT

This Eastern European classic is wonderful nourishing meal to share. All those healthy ingredients are cleansing and great for the waning moon phase, but honestly, I'd have it anytime. Who wouldn't want to enjoy immune-boosting cruciferous vegetables in a gorgeous bowl of soup? It can be served hot or cold depending on the weather. Smacznego!

PICTURED ON PAGE 46

SERVES 6–8

- 1 onion, diced
- 2 teaspoons caraway seeds
- 2 tablespoons olive oil
- 4 cloves garlic, chopped or minced
- 2 carrots, peeled and thinly julienned or quartered
- 4 beetroot, peeled and diced
- ¼ red or white cabbage, chopped
- 2 medium potatoes, peeled and cut into small cubes
- 2 bay leaves
- salt and pepper
- 2 teaspoons rapadura sugar or rice syrup (optional)
- 80 ml apple cider vinegar

To serve

Sour Cream (see page 207), fresh dill and cornbread or crusty bread

In a big beautiful pot, fry the onion and caraway seeds gently in the olive oil until the onion softens. Add the garlic, followed by the rest of the vegetables and stir for a few minutes.

Add 1.2 litres water, bay leaves, a pinch of salt and the sweetener, and cook on low heat until all the vegetables are soft.

Add the vinegar, salt and pepper to taste, and let the soup sit for a while for the flavours to infuse.

You can eat the soup straight away but it becomes even better the next day when those flavours have developed deeply.

Serve in good company with fresh dill and vegan sour cream (plain or flavoured with horseradish). Some kind of bread is a must – cornbread is especially good.

NOTE Borscht will keep in an airtight container in the fridge for 4 days. It also freezes well.

VEGAN RAMEN *in* A CREAMY BROTH

Ramen is one of my favourite foods, and we eat it a LOT in our household, so it made sense that I set out to create the perfect vegan ramen. The great thing about ramen is that you can add whatever Asian vegetables you have lying around! I often find myself adding other vegetables that are due to expire, so get creative with this, and enjoy.

SERVES 2

- 500 ml vegetable stock
- 2–3 tablespoons olive oil
- 100 g firm tofu, chopped into small cubes
- 3 tablespoons soy sauce
- 1 teaspoon dark miso paste
- 2 teaspoons ginger, grated
- 2 teaspoons garlic, grated
- 1 spring onion, the white part sliced for frying, dark green part thinly sliced for garnish
- 100 g fresh shiitake mushrooms, halved
- 4–6 bok choy leaves and stalks, cut into bite-size pieces
- 2 servings ramen noodles (packaged or fresh)
- 3 tablespoons tahini
- 2 teaspoons rice vinegar
- ½ cup bean sprouts
- 1 tablespoon sriracha, plus more for garnish

Pour the vegetable stock into a saucepan over low heat to slowly heat up while you prepare the other ingredients.

Heat 1 tablespoon of the oil in a small pan over medium–high heat. Add tofu and cook, stirring occasionally, until golden brown and crispy.

Meanwhile, in a small bowl combine 1 tablespoon of the soy sauce with the miso paste and stir well to dissolve.

Reduce the heat to medium, push the tofu to one side of the pan and fry the ginger and garlic until cooked through. Stir the tofu back in. Add the soy sauce–miso paste mixture. Allow the liquid to boil off and fry the tofu for a couple more minutes to allow it to crisp up again in the paste. Remove to a plate.

Add another 1–2 tablespoons of the oil to the pan and allow to heat up. Add the sliced white part of the spring onion and the shiitake mushrooms. Gently fry them together for 5–10 minutes until they are golden brown. Remove to a plate.

Add the bok choy to the pan and fry until the leaves are wilted and stalks are crisp-tender.

Meanwhile, bring a saucepan of water to the boil. Add the noodles and cook according to the packet instructions.

In a bowl, combine the tahini, 2 tablespoons of soy sauce, rice vinegar and sriracha. Mix well, add to the hot stock and stir well to combine.

Pour the stock into serving bowls, then add the noodles. Top with the vegetables, tofu, bean sprouts and thinly sliced green part of the spring onion. Serve extra sriracha on the side for drizzling over the top.

EASY-PEASY TURMERIC LAKSA *with* TEMPEH

This simple laksa is the bee's knees. It has an exotic taste with big punches of flavour that impress guests. A little special something about this laksa: it was the first thing I cooked for my now partner in our very early days. Two-and-a-half years and one little baby later, we're more in love than ever. I caught my soulmate with this powerful dish, so be careful!

SERVES 4

Tempeh

- 1 block tempeh
- 2 tablespoons tamari
- 2 tablespoons peanut butter
- juice of 1 lime
- pinch of salt
- dash each of coconut oil and sesame oil

FOR THE TEMPEH, cut the tempeh block through the middle to make thinner slices, then cut diagonally into triangles.

Mix all the marinade ingredients together in a medium bowl, adding lime juice to taste – add more for a punchier flavour – and enough oil to make a smooth paste. Fold in the tempeh. Leave sit for at least 30 minutes. Even better, marinate it the day before and leave in the fridge overnight.

Preheat the oven to 200°C.

Spread the tempeh on an oven tray along with its marinade, and cook in the oven for 25–30 minutes until nice and golden. Keep an eye on it and turn the pieces over after 15 minutes.

Laksa

- 1 teaspoon coconut oil
- 1 teaspoon sesame oil
- 1 tablespoon ground turmeric (or fresh, grated)
- 2 tablespoons ground ginger (or fresh, grated)
- ½ teaspoon garlic powder (or fresh, crushed)
- broccoli, cut into small florets
- cauliflower, cut into small florets
- 4 fresh shiitake mushrooms (or button)
- zucchini, halved lengthways, then cut in ½ cm wedges on an angle
- dash of tamari
- rice noodles, according to how hungry you are
- snow peas, trimmed, then sliced on an angle
- 1 x 400 ml can coconut milk
- 1 heaped teaspoon vegan miso paste
- salt and pepper
- lime and fresh coriander, to serve

FOR THE LAKSA, heat the oils in a wok over high heat. Once hot, add the spices and let the flavour release. Add the broccoli, cauliflower, mushrooms and ¼ cup water to help it all cook. After about 15 minutes, add the zucchini. Throw in a good dash of tamari.

Meanwhile, cook the rice noodles according to packet instructions. When cooked, drain and set aside.

When the vegies are almost done, add the snow peas, turn down the heat and stir in the coconut milk.

When the coconut milk is warmed through, turn off the heat and stir in the miso paste. Season to taste with tamari, salt, pepper and lime juice.

Heap the noodles into bowls, add the vegies and soup, and top with the tempeh. Add coriander, a squeeze of lime and more tamari to taste.

NOTES The laksa and tempeh will keep in airtight containers in the fridge for 4 days. Store separately so the soup doesn't make the tempeh and noodles soggy. ● The cooked rice noodles will keep in an airtight container for 1 day. ● You can also freeze the laksa. ● You can substitute almost everything: tofu instead of tempeh; Thai basil instead of coriander; rice, quinoa or vegie noodles instead of rice noodles. ● Add lentils or mung beans if you want a bit more protein.

HEARTY WARMING MINESTRONE

This is a one-pot super easy meal that tastes even better the next day as the flavours develop. The recipe is based on my Italian mother-in-law's soup and is much loved by our family. Use whatever vegies you have on hand.

SERVES 4–5

- 2 carrots
- 1 large onion
- 1 stalk celery
- 1 medium potato
- 2 tablespoons olive oil
- 1–2 cloves garlic, finely chopped
- 1 tablespoon tomato paste
- 1–1.5 litres vegetable stock
- 1 x 400 g can diced tomatoes
- ½ cup split peas
- 1 cup frozen baby peas
- 1 cup vegan red wine
- 1 x 400 g can white beans or chickpeas
- 2 cups of elbow pasta
- 1 handful spinach leaves

To serve

- crusty bread and vegan parmesan

Peel and dice all the vegies.

Heat the oil in a heavy based saucepan. Add the onion, carrot, celery and garlic and cook on medium heat until soft and translucent, but don't brown. Add the tomato paste and cook for about a minute.

Add the stock and potato and bring to boil.

Add the tinned tomatoes, split peas, frozen peas, red wine and beans or chickpeas and bring to the boil once again. Reduce heat and simmer for 30 minutes.

Add the pasta and cook gently for a further 15–20 minutes until pasta is soft. Add the spinach and season with salt and pepper.

Serve with some crusty bread and vegan parmesan.

NOTES The soup will keep in an airtight container in the fridge for a few days (if it lasts that long!). ● Make a big batch and freeze some for later. ● Use a couple of vegie stock cubes or Massel stock powder. Or make your own stock using the recipe on page 213. ● Make your own Vegan Parmesan using one of the easy recipes on page 205.

LEEK CHOWDER

This is Pam's other favourite recipe, after Sweet & Sour Tofu Balls (see page 33). The original recipe came from my eldest daughter, Cathy, but it included butter, milk and chicken (!) so I converted it to be vegan

SERVES 3

- 2 large or 3 medium leeks, chopped
- 2 large potatoes, peeled and chopped
- 2 large or 3 medium carrots, chopped
- 2 teaspoons Massel stock powder in 2 cups water
- 420 g can corn kernels, rinsed and drained
- 40 g vegan butter (I use Nuttelex Buttery)
- ¾ cup plain flour
- 1 cup soy milk

Combine leeks, potatoes, carrots and stock in a large saucepan and bring to the boil. Let simmer for 25 minutes or until carrots soften. Add the corn kernels.

Meanwhile, in a second saucepan, melt the butter over medium heat and add the flour, stirring to make a paste. Slowly add the milk, stirring constantly until the sauce thickens, then add the leek mixture. Turn the heat to low and continue to cook for 5 minutes, stirring continually to prevent the chowder from catching.

Enjoy!

NOTE Leftovers will keep in an airtight container in the fridge for a day.

A BOWL of SUNSHINE

It's not everyday that a piglet gets a soup dedicated to her but Sunny warms the hearts of all who meet her, just like this nourishing soup will warm yours on a chilly day. Even on the darkest days Sunny is there to lift our spirits with her cheeky antics and zoomies around her paddock.

SERVES 3–4

- 1 yellow capsicum
- olive oil spray
- 3–4 pieces of corn on the cob, fresh or frozen
- 1 tablespoon olive oil
- ½ brown onion, chopped finely
- 1 litre vegetable stock
- 500 g fresh or frozen sweetcorn kernels
- 3 cm piece of fresh turmeric, peeled and grated, or 2 teaspoons ground turmeric
- sea salt and black pepper

To serve

- fresh coriander and lime

Preheat the oven to 200°C fan-forced. Line an oven tray with foil.

Remove the core and seeds of the capsicum and cut the flesh into wide strips. Spray lightly on both sides with olive oil and place on the prepared baking tray skin-side up. Cook in the hot oven for 25 minutes until starting to blister but not blackened.

Steam the pieces of corn on the cob for about 20 minutes until tender, if using fresh corn. If using frozen corn cobs, cook according to packet instructions.

In a large pot, sweat the onion with the olive oil and a generous splash of water until the onion is transparent – you might need to add a little more water to keep it steamy.

Add the stock, the corn kernels and turmeric and bring to the boil. Reduce the heat, cover and simmer for about 20 minutes (a bit longer for fresh kernels).

Reserve about a cup of the soup with whole corn kernels, and blend the rest with the capsicum until smooth. Return the whole corn kernels to the blended soup, heat through and season to taste.

Serve in bowls with one piece of corn on the cob per person, a squeeze of lime and coriander.

NOTES The soup will keep in an airtight container for up to 3 days in the fridge. It can also be frozen for up to 3 months. ● This soup is great with smashed avocado on toast, a squeeze of lime and a little chilli. ● Make your own vegie stock (see page 213).

'Knowing I am *saving* animals every day keeps my *soul* happy.'

TAYLAH JADE BOURKE

Recipe list

SHIITAKE BANH MI

OUR SMALL PLANET BURGER

MUSHROOM GYROS *with* TZATZIKI

THAI FISHLESS CAKES *with* PEANUT SAUCE

BETTER-FOR-YOU PAD THAI

ZUCCHINI PANCAKES, JAPANESE STYLE

ROASTED JACKFRUIT SHAWARMA

TOFU LARB

SPAGHETTI *and* NEATBALLS IN NAPOLI SAUCE

GRANDMA BETTY'S MAC *and* CHEESE *with* VEGIES

SPANAKOPITA

MUSHROOM *and* GUINNESS PIES

CRUNCHY OVEN CHIPS

BELLA'S BEST SHEPHERD'S PIE

VEGANISE

it

Never miss out
with classics
made vegan

SHIITAKE BANH MI

This is my Japanese adaptation of a recipe that originally used strictly Vietnamese flavourings. It's fresh and light and one of those dishes you can serve to anyone – vegan or not – and they'll want the recipe! You can tweak the seasonings and flavours to suit yourself or the season.

SERVES 4

- 2 tablespoons brown rice vinegar
- 4 tablespoons mirin
- 1 teaspoon sugar
- pinch of sea salt
- 1 medium carrot, peeled and cut into matchsticks
- 1 small Lebanese cucumber, seeded and cut into matchsticks
- 500 g fresh shiitake mushrooms, washed and patted dry
- 8 cloves garlic, peeled and thinly sliced
- sea salt
- freshly cracked black pepper
- chilli and coriander-infused olive oil
- ¼ cup light miso paste
- ¼ cup mushroom soy sauce (or shiitake tsuyu)
- 2 tablespoons lime juice
- 2 tablespoons sesame oil
- 2 cm piece ginger, peeled and grated
- 4 banh mi bread rolls

To serve

Kewpie No Egg Mayonnaise, sprigs of fresh coriander or Vietnamese mint, pickled ginger, fresh red chilli

Preheat the oven to 180°C.

In a small mixing bowl, combine brown rice vinegar, 1 tablespoon of the mirin, sugar and sea salt and stir to dissolve. Add carrot and cucumber and toss to mix well. Set aside.

Prepare a baking tray that is large enough to spread the mushrooms and garlic in a single layer by spraying lightly with non-stick cooking spray.

Remove the mushroom stems and set aside. Thinly slice the mushroom caps. Using your fingers, shred the reserved mushroom stems. Spread the mushrooms and garlic on the tray. Season with sea salt and pepper and drizzle generously with the chilli-coriander olive oil. Toss until the mushrooms are well coated. Bake for 15 minutes.

Meanwhile, in a small mixing bowl stir together the remaining mirin, the miso paste, soy sauce, lime juice, sesame oil and grated ginger. Pour mixture over mushrooms and garlic and stir gently to coat. Bake for a further 15 minutes. Remove from the oven and drizzle with additional lime juice, if desired.

To serve, cut the rolls in half and spread each side lightly with the mayonnaise. Top with the mushroom mixture, pickled carrots and cucumber, coriander or Vietnamese mint, a few slices of pickled ginger and chopped chillies, if it's not already spicy enough for your liking. Serve immediately.

NOTES The cooked mushrooms will keep in an airtight container in the fridge for 2 days. • Kewpie No Egg Mayonnaise is available online from The Cruelty Free Shop – it's worth tracking down!

SANDY & BILL EATON

OUR SMALL PLANET BURGER

During the 1980s, I loved going to the Good Earth restaurants in Los Gatos and Cupertino, California. I was sad to see them close. Eventually I was inspired to recreate their much-loved Small Planet Burger. We make two batches at a time, cook them up and freeze them for quick meals later on

MAKES 8 BURGERS

- oil, for frying
- ¼ cup brown onion, chopped
- ⅓ cup mushrooms, sliced
- 1 x 420 g can adzuki beans
- 1 x 420 g can pinto beans
- ¼ cup sesame seeds, toasted or raw
- ¼ cup sunflower seeds, toasted or raw
- ¼ cup cashews, toasted or raw
- ½ cup walnuts or pine nuts
- 1 cup chopped vegetables such as capsicum, carrot, zucchini, beet greens
- 1 tablespoon tamari or liquid aminos
- breadcrumbs or flour to thicken, if needed

To serve

- burger buns, vegan mayo and fillings such as lettuce, tomato, red onion and pickles

Heat a little oil in a frying pan over medium heat and sauté the onions. Add the mushrooms after a couple of minutes and cook till softened. Cool.

Drain the beans, saving the liquid from the pinto beans in case you need it later to moisten the patty mixture. Combine the beans in a large bowl and mash well. Add the mushrooms and onion.

Combine the bean mixture with the seeds and nuts in a food processor. If you are toasting the seeds, leave to cool before adding. Add vegetables, tamari or liquid aminos. Process until smooth.

Place the processed mixture in a large bowl. Add breadcrumbs or flour to thicken mixture – you need to be able to form patties that are moist but hold together. If the mixture feels too thick or too dry, add a little of the saved pinto bean juice.

Form mixture into 8 good-sized patties. You can leave them for a few hours in the fridge to firm up if you like.

Heat a little oil in a frying pan over medium heat and cook the patties for 4–5 minutes or until brown. The longer they cook undisturbed, the better they will stick together. Turn over carefully and fry until cooked all the way through. You can also bake them, lightly sprayed with oil, for about 25 minutes at 180°C until slightly crusty on top.

To serve, split and lightly toast the burger buns. Spread with vegan mayo, add patties and top with lettuce, tomato, red onion and pickle.

NOTES The cooked patties, or the mixture, will keep in an airtight container in the fridge for a couple of days. • Separate the cooked patties with baking paper when freezing. • Swap adzuki beans for red kidney beans, and pinto beans for borlotti beans.

MUSHROOM GYROS *with* TZATZIKI

I found this recipe on the Brand New Vegan blog a few years ago, and have been making my version of it ever since. I love gyros, and this recipe nails the flavours. It's fantastic for entertaining as it looks a lot more complicated than it is. It's also great with a Greek salad or roasted potatoes.

SERVES 4

Tzatziki

- 1 Lebanese cucumber, grated
- 1 cup Coyo natural yoghurt
- 1–2 cloves garlic (depending on how garlicky you like it), crushed
- juice of 1 lemon
- pinch of salt

Marinade

- 1 teaspoon dried oregano
- ½ teaspoon garlic powder
- ½ teaspoon onion powder
- ½ teaspoon ground cumin
- ½ teaspoon liquid smoke
- ¼ teaspoon black pepper
- 1/8 teaspoon ground cloves
- ¼ cup soy sauce or liquid aminos

Filling

- 500 g portobello mushrooms, sliced
- 1 tablespoon olive oil

To serve

- pita bread, tomatoes, lettuce and cucumber

FOR THE TZATZIKI, lightly salt the cucumber and set aside in a colander for 5–10 minutes to drain some of the liquid away. Then simply mix all ingredients together in a small bowl; I find Coyo yoghurt a little on the sweeter side, so adjust the salt and lemon juice to your liking.

FOR THE GYROS, preheat oven to 180°C.

Whisk all the marinade ingredients together in a large bowl. Mix mushrooms with the marinade until well covered.

Heat oil in a large pan over medium heat, and sauté the mushrooms until they have reduced in size and are cooked through.

Transfer mushrooms to a tray lined with baking paper – this should be big enough to allow a single layer of mushrooms. Cook in the oven for 10 minutes, or until the mushrooms are slightly crispy (or to your liking).

When you're ready to serve, heat the pita breads in a pan for a minute or two each side, or use a microwave.

Assemble gyros by layering the mushrooms, tomatoes, lettuce and cucumber on the pita breads, and don't forget the tzatziki over the top!

NOTES The filling will keep in an airtight container in the fridge for 2–3 days. • Make the tzatziki a day ahead for the best result – the flavours of the garlic and lemon juice will develop over time.

THAI FISHLESS CAKES *with* PEANUT SAUCE

I came up with this recipe as a gluten-free finger food option for a function. Easy to eat with one hand! The fishless cakes also work well with sweet chilli sauce, while the versatile peanut sauce is great warmed with a little extra stock and poured over roasted vegies.

SERVES 4

Curry paste

- 2 stalks lemongrass, outer layer and tough parts removed
- 1 red banana chilli
- 1 large piece of ginger, peeled
- 4 cloves garlic, peeled
- 1 small shallot, peeled
- roots from 1 small bunch coriander, well washed
- 4 kaffir lime leaves
- 1 tablespoon curry powder
- 1 tablespoon turmeric
- ½ cup water

Fishless cakes

- 300g firm tofu, roughly chopped
- 1 teaspoon vegan miso paste
- 1 tablespoon tamari
- ½ cup chopped spring onion
- ½ cup chopped coriander leaves
- juice of 2 limes
- 1 teaspoon vegan fish sauce (optional)
- 1 cup cornflour

Peanut sauce

See Easy Peanut Sauce, page 210

FOR THE CURRY PASTE, roughly chop all the ingredients and blend in a food processor until smooth. Place in a saucepan and cook on low heat until the liquid has absorbed.

FOR THE FISHLESS CAKES, place all ingredients as well as the prepared curry paste in a food processor and process until mix resembles breadcrumbs. Rest in the fridge for an hour, then shape into small cakes. Heat a little oil in a non-stick pan over low heat and shallow-fry until golden brown each side.

Serve fishless cakes with a generous amount of peanut sauce.

NOTES Leftover fishless cakes will keep in an airtight container in the fridge for 5 days, separated by greaseproof paper. Reheat in the oven. They can be frozen in the same way. • Vegan fish sauce is a wonderful sauce made from fermented mushrooms, found at Asian grocers. • The fishless cakes also make delicious burgers with a crunchy Asian slaw and avocado.

BETTER-FOR-YOU PAD THAI

We tried a few different vegan versions of this classic Thai noodle dish, and ended up with this saucy, spicy and flavour-filled pad thai that quickly became a favourite dish! It's also a lot healthier than a takeaway pad thai, so you can enjoy a good portion size! PICTURED ON PAGE 72

SERVES 2 HUNGRY PEOPLE

- 1 tablespoon olive oil
- 1 white onion, diced
- 1 carrot, diced
- 250 g tofu, cut into 1 cm dice
- 1 small red capsicum, diced
- 1 zucchini, diced or spiralised
- 200 g flat rice noodles
- ¼ cup unsalted peanuts
- ½ cup fresh coriander, chopped
- lime wedges, to serve

Sauce

- 3 tablespoons sambal paste (or chilli sauce)
- 3 tablespoons tamarind puree
- 3 tablespoons sesame oil
- 3 tablespoons mirin
- 3 tablespoons rice wine vinegar
- 3 tablespoons soy sauce
- 1 tablespoon lemon juice
- 6 cloves garlic, minced
- 3 tablespoons sesame oil
- 3 tablespoons maple syrup

Combine all the sauce ingredients in a bowl – it should make about 1 cup of sauce. Use approximately ¼ cup of the sauce to marinate the tofu, and place in the fridge for 30 minutes.

Heat oil in a pan and sauté onion for 5 minutes. Add carrot, tofu and another ¼ cup of the sauce. Cook over medium heat for another 5 minutes.

Add capsicum and zucchini, and cook for a further 5 minutes. Set aside.

Meanwhile, soak the rice noodles in boiling water for 10 minutes, or cook according to packet instructions. Once drained, fry noodles in the remaining sauce before mixing with the vegetables and tofu. Stir in half of the chopped peanuts and half the chopped coriander.

Serve hot, topped with remaining peanuts, coriander leaves and lime wedges

NOTE Best served freshly cooked, but leftovers will keep in an airtight container in the fridge for up to 3 days.

ZUCCHINI PANCAKES, JAPANESE STYLE

This is a recipe of my own creation, inspired by traditional Japanese okonomiyaki. Zucchini is the star of this dish. Make small pancakes for a quick lunch or an easy snack – just be careful bringing these to parties as they will vanish in seconds and you will be pestered for the recipe by vegans and non-vegans of alike!

SERVES 2

- ¾ cup flour
- ¼ cup chickpea flour
- ½ teaspoon baking powder
- 2 tablespoons nutritional yeast
- 1 teaspoon kala namak (black salt)
- pinch of black pepper
- 2 spring onions, chopped
- 1 clove garlic, minced
- 200 g carrots, peeled and grated
- 300 g zucchini, grated
- 2 tablespoons sherry (optional)
- sunflower oil (or oil of your choice)

To serve

vegan mayonnaise, hoisin sauce, pickled ginger, sliced spring onions, sliced nori, sesame seeds and a simple lettuce salad

Combine all ingredients in a large bowl with ½ cup water and mix well.

Heat oil in a frying pan over medium heat, and cook half the batter until golden on both sides. Turn once during cooking. Repeat with remaining mixture.

Serve with generous drizzles of mayonnaise and hoisin sauce, and perhaps a simple lettuce salad. To make the dish really impressive, sprinkle with sliced nori, pickled ginger, sliced spring onion and sesame seeds.

NOTES Leftovers will keep in an airtight container in the fridge for 2–3 days. Reheat in the microwave. ● Kewpie No Egg Mayonnaise is available online from The Cruelty Free Shop. ● This is a great low-budget recipe because zucchinis are affordable and available all year round. They're also quick and easy to prepare with very little waste.

ROASTED JACKFRUIT SHAWARMA

I am a recipe developer and food blogger and I'm the only vegan in a family of omnivores. I try and create recipes that my meat-eating family will also enjoy so I only have to cook plant-based. This messy and addictive Middle Eastern wrap is a family favourite. PICTURED ON PAGE 72

SERVES 6

Shawarma 'meat'

- 550 g canned young jackfruit in brine
- 400 g cooked chickpeas
- juice of 1 lemon
- ¼ cup good quality olive oil
- 3 cloves garlic, minced
- 1 teaspoon sea salt
- 1 teaspoon freshly ground black pepper
- 2 teaspoons ground cumin
- ¾ teaspoon smoked paprika
- ½ teaspoon ground cinnamon
- ¼ teaspoon turmeric (optional)
- 1 large red onion, finely sliced
- 2 tablespoons parsley, finely chopped

Lemon tahini sauce

- 1 clove garlic
- ¼ cup lemon juice
- ⅓ cup tahini
- ½ teaspoon sea salt
- ½ teaspoon ground cumin or sumac

To serve

- 6 pita breads
- 1½ cups lettuce, thinly sliced
- 2 tomatoes, sliced
- ⅓ cup hummus
- pickles (optional)

FOR THE 'MEAT', drain the brine from the jackfruit. Thinly slice each triangle lengthways and pop the pieces in a large bowl. Add the remaining meat ingredients and stir to combine. Cover with a clean cloth and refrigerate overnight or for at least 2 hours.

Preheat the oven to 190°C.

Remove the marinated jackfruit from the fridge and spread it out over a roasting pan or tray. Roast for 35 to 40 minutes or until some of the jackfruit edges are starting to char. Set aside.

FOR THE SAUCE, blend all the ingredients with 3–4 tablespoons water until smooth. Add more water if needed to thin the sauce out.

TO SERVE, warm each pita gently in a dry pan over medium heat for a minute or two, turning halfway through. Lay each pita on a plate and smear with a good dollop of hummus. Add sliced lettuce and tomato followed by a good handful of the roasted jackfruit mixture. Add pickles (optional) and drizzle with lemon tahini sauce. Fold the bottom of the pita up and then roll from the side to make a wrap.

Dig in!

NOTES The filling will keep in an airtight container in the fridge for up to 5 days, and freezes well for up to 2 months. ● The shawarma can also be served with rice and a good drizzle of Lemon Tahini Sauce.

TOFU LARB

I think all too often, people throw in the towel before their vegan journey has even begun. But when we shift our mindsets and recognise that we're all in this together, that animals are here with us and not for us, veganism becomes not only manageable but deeply fulfilling. An inclusive world of limitless possibilities suddenly opens up, and it can be downright magical. **PICTURED ON PAGE 73**

SERVES 2

- ¼ cup white rice
- vegetable oil, for frying
- 1 x 450 g pack firm tofu, cubed
- 200 g mushrooms, sliced
- ½ onion, thinly sliced (optional)
- ½ lemon, juiced
- mint leaves, to taste
- mushroom soy sauce or other mild soy sauce
- 1 teaspoon ground chilli

To serve

- quinoa or rice
- lettuce leaves

Toast grains of rice with a small amount of vegetable oil over low heat until brown, then grind with a mortar and pestle. Set aside.

Heat vegetable oil in a frying pan over high heat, and cook the tofu for 8 minutes or until brown, turning a few times.

Add mushrooms and onion (if using) to the pan, and cook for an additional 5 minutes.

Mix in the ground rice, lemon juice, some fresh mint, mushroom soy sauce and chilli.

Serve over quinoa or rice with lettuce leaves – easy *and* delicious!

FOLLOWING PAGE (clockwise from top right):

Grandma Betty's Mac and Cheese with Vegies, 75
Tofu Larb
Better-for-you Pad Thai, 67
Roasted Jackfruit Shawarma, 70
Spaghetti and Neatballs in Napoli Sauce, 74

SPAGHETTI *and* NEATBALLS IN NAPOLI SAUCE

This is an easy and delicious lunch or dinner meal from Animals Australia – their VegKit.com is a great source of vegan recipes. The method is easily adapted for those who use a Thermomix. **PICTURED ON PAGE 72**

SERVES 2

Neatballs

3 teaspoons ground flaxseed

1 x 400 g tin brown lentils, rinsed and drained

1 cup almond meal

⅓ cup breadcrumbs

1 tablespoon tamari

¼ teaspoon chilli flakes

300 g spaghetti

1 tablespoon extra virgin olive oil

Napoli sauce

1 tablespoon extra virgin olive oil

2 cloves garlic, chopped

1 x 400 g tin crushed tomatoes, blended until smooth

1 tablespoon tomato paste

½ cup vegetable stock

½ teaspoon brown sugar

1 teaspoon mixed dried herbs (I use dried oregano)

basil leaves, torn, to taste

To serve

¼ cup basil leaves, to serve

vegan parmesan (see page 202) or nutritional yeast

FOR THE SAUCE, heat oil in a small saucepan over medium heat and sauté garlic for 1–2 minutes until soft. Add all other sauce ingredients and simmer for 10 minutes or until thick.

FOR THE BALLS, first make a flax egg by combining the ground flaxseed with 1½ tablespoons water. Set aside for 15 minutes in the fridge to thicken. Process lentils in a food processor for about 20 seconds. Add flax egg, almond meal, breadcrumbs, tamari and chilli flakes, and process until well combined. Roll mixture into balls.

Heat oil in a large frying pan over medium heat and fry the balls for 4–5 minutes until browned all over, turning frequently to prevent them sticking to the pan.

Add the sauce to the pan, stirring gently so the balls are covered in sauce.

Cook spaghetti in a large saucepan of salted boiling water for 8–10 minutes or until al dente. Check packet instructions. Drain.

TO SERVE, divide the spaghetti between bowls, arrange the balls on top and pour over the sauce. Served topped with basil leaves and vegan parmesan or nutritional yeast.

NOTES Neatballs and sauce will keep in an airtight container in the fridge for at least 3 days. They can also be frozen. • Edamame spaghetti (or any vegie noodles) is a great serving alternative to pasta. • Consider omitting the chilli if cooking for kids.

GRANDMA BETTY'S MAC *and* CHEESE *with* VEGIES

Hester and I love to veganise our old favourite meals, so we never feel like we're missing out on anything. This recipe is adapted from Hester's mum's famous mac and cheese, which was a family favourite growing up. This new vegan version gets the tick of approval, too. I have coeliac disease, so we always cook gluten free, but of course the recipe works just as well with gluten. Our pro tip is to add tofu bacon (see page 212 to make your own) for protein and extra yumminess. **PICTURED ON PAGE 73**

SERVES 4

- 250 g gluten-free pasta
- 2 cups of chopped vegies (we love to add greens like broccoli, spinach and kale)
- 60 g vegan butter (we use Nuttelex)
- 3 tablespoons gluten-free all-purpose flour
- 2 cups plant-based milk (we use Vitasoy Soy Milky)
- 200 g vegan cheese (see note)
- ⅓ cup nutritional yeast
- 1 teaspoon mustard
- salt and pepper, to taste
- Tofu Bacon (optional), see page 215
- green salad or steamed green vegies, to serve

Cook pasta according to packet instructions, adding vegetables halfway through. Drain pasta and vegies and set aside.

In a large saucepan, melt the vegan butter. Whisk in the flour and cook for 1 minute, taking care not to let it burn.

Slowly add the milk and keep whisking to form a smooth, runny sauce.

Add the vegan cheese, nutritional yeast and mustard and allow the cheese to melt in. Once melted, add salt and pepper to taste, and mix the pasta and vegies through the sauce. Add tofu bacon if using.

Easy-peasy!

Serve with a leafy green salad or steamed green vegies.

NOTES Leftovers will keep in an airtight container in the fridge for 3–5 days. It can be frozen whole or in portions. • For the vegan cheese, we find a combination of Biocheese cheddar and pizza shreds works well, but any cheese you like will do the trick. • If you like crunchy bits on your mac and cheese, finish it off by baking in a hot oven for 10 minutes or so, just until it's browned.

SPANAKOPITA

Before I went vegan, I used to love making a spinach and feta pie. So I developed this recipe, which is really tasty, very easy, and probably healthier than the original! It's a very forgiving recipe – the quantities of spinach and tofu don't matter too much either way.

SERVES 4

- 1 x 250 g packet frozen spinach, defrosted
- 1 x 450 g packet firm tofu
- 1 teaspoon salt
- ½ teaspoon black pepper
- 2 teaspoons Dijon mustard
- 1 bunch dill
- 3 spring onions, finely sliced
- 8 sheets filo pastry, defrosted
- olive oil or oil spray
- salad, to serve

Preheat your oven to 180°C.

Prepare a baking dish (approximately 20 cm x 30 cm) by spraying well with oil, or lining with baking paper.

Squeeze as much liquid as possible out of the defrosted spinach, otherwise the pastry will go very soggy and the filling will be too wet.

Crumble the packet of tofu into small pieces. In a large bowl, mix the tofu with the spinach, salt, pepper and mustard. Finely chop half the bunch of dill, and add to the mixture with the spring onions. Mix well so all ingredients are thoroughly combined.

At this stage, taste and add more dill if you love the flavour, and more salt and pepper if required. I like to add plenty of salt to replicate the feta flavour, but adjust according to your personal taste.

Lay down 4 sheets of filo to cover the base of the baking dish, spoon the filling over it, then add the final 4 sheets on top, brushing or spraying the top with oil.

If you want to make it a little bit more fancy, or easier to serve individually, take 2 sheets of filo laid on top of each other. Take a quarter of the mixture and spread it out in a tube shape diagonally across the pastry, then roll the pastry around it like a big, long sausage roll. Carefully coil the tube like a snail shell so you have a spiral. Place the spiral on the tray, and repeat three times with remaining ingredients. Brush or spray with oil.

Place in the preheated oven and bake for 25–30 minutes, or until the pastry is golden.

Serve with a salad or any of your favourite sides.

MUSHROOM *and* GUINNESS PIES

It's official – good things come to vegans who wait, and all Guinness beers are now suitable for vegans in draught, bottle and can form. So that means we can make a hearty Guinness pie. Bottoms up to that – there's nothing more comforting than a home-baked pie. To deepen the flavours, I recommend preparing the filling a day or two before you make the pies.

MAKES 6–12, DEPENDING ON SIZE

Filling

- 2 cups dried porcini mushrooms
- 1 large brown onion, diced
- 2 tablespoons olive oil
- 1¼ teaspoons salt
- 4 cloves garlic, minced
- 1 cup cremini mushrooms, thinly sliced
- 3 stalks celery, thinly sliced
- 3 carrots, thinly diced
- 2 cups russet potatoes, peeled and diced
- 2 teaspoons dried thyme
- 1 teaspoon dried rosemary
- 1¼ cups Guinness beer
- 2 tablespoons tomato paste
- 2 teaspoons sugar
- freshly ground black pepper
- salt
- 3 cups vegan beef stock (I use Massel)
- ⅓ cup plain flour

FOR THE STEW, place the dried porcini mushrooms in a bowl. Cover with boiling water and let sit for approximately 15 minutes.

Heat the oil in a pan and sauté the onions, adding the salt. Cook for about 5 minutes until onions turn translucent. Add garlic, and cook for a further minute.

Add the cremini mushrooms (but not the porcinis just yet), celery, carrot, potatoes, thyme and rosemary. Sauté for 5 minutes, or until the mushrooms release moisture and brown slightly.

Add the Guinness, tomato paste and sugar, season with pepper and salt and bring to the boil. The liquid should reduce in about 3 minutes.

Drain and chop the porcini mushrooms and add to the pan. Add the stock, cover and bring to a full boil for 5 minutes or so. Reduce heat and simmer uncovered until all vegetables are fork-tender, about 15 minutes.

Gradually whisk a cup of cold water into the flour until no lumps are left. Slowly add to the pot, stirring well as you go. Cook for 5 minutes or so, until the stew thickens.

Take off the heat and let the stew cool for about 15 minutes. Note that the flavours will develop further if the filling is left overnight.

CONTINUED >

Pastry

6 sheets vegan shortcrust pastry (for base)

3 sheets vegan puff pastry (for top)

1 tablespoon vegan butter (I use Nuttelex)

To serve

mashed potato, mushy peas, vegan gravy, barbecue or tomato sauce

TO MAKE THE PIES, leave the puff pastry and shortcrust pastry on the bench to defrost. Check the packet instructions.

Preheat oven to 220°C.

Oil 6 standard or 12 small pie dishes and line each with the thawed shortcrust pastry. (You can also buy disposable aluminium pie trays.) Fill each pie case with the pie filling.

Using a cutter, or ramekin or saucer, cut circles out of the thawed puff pastry that will be the right size to fit over the top of the pie. Place the pastry rounds on top to cover the pie mixture and use a lightly floured fork to press the edges together. Use a small sharp knife to make 2 slits in the top of each pastry lid.

If you're feeling creative, cut out a few shapes from the leftover pastry with a biscuit cutter and put them on top of the pies. Brush the tops lightly with a little melted vegan butter and bake for 35–40 minutes or until golden.

Set aside for 10 minutes to cool slightly, then remove from the tins.

Serve hot with mashed potato, mushy peas and vegan gravy. Or you can have them the Aussie way with either barbecue or tomato sauce.

NOTES These pies are best eaten on the day they are made. You can store them in an airtight container in the fridge for up to 5 days. ● The pies freeze well in sealed freezer bags for up to 2 months. Thaw overnight in the fridge and reheat in an oven preheated to 180°C for 20–25 minutes. ● Guinness can sometimes add a slightly bitter taste to the stew, so a small amount of sugar can be added to round out the flavour. ● Cremini mushrooms are brown baby portobello mushrooms. If you can't find them, use white ones instead. ● Caramelised onions, miso and beef stock make a great vegan gravy, or try Amazing Gravy on page 211.

CRUNCHY OVEN CHIPS

These chips are a great accompaniment to a meal, and are also yummy as the star of the show with sauce or relish. They're easy to make and you can control how much oil and salt you use on a food that's normally considered very unhealthy. Most vegans will have the secret ingredient I use here: nooch (nutritional yeast). But you might not have discovered how good it is for seasoning homemade chips!

SERVES 2 PEOPLE

- 2–3 large potatoes, around 575 grams
- 2 tablespoons olive oil
- ½ teaspoon black salt
- 1 tablespoon nutritional yeast
- generous pinch of pepper
- ½ tablespoon dried herbs (optional)

Preheat oven to 180 degrees. Lined an oven tray with baking paper.

Peel the potatoes and slice into chips, 1.5–2 cm thick. (Reduce cooking time for thinner chips.)

Put the chips in a large bowl. Mix with olive oil, black salt, nutritional yeast and pepper until all chips are covered. Add dried herbs prior to mixing if desired.

Put the chips on the oven tray, making sure they're not touching each other.

Cook for 20 minutes, then turn chips over and cook for another 20 minutes.

Take out from oven and serve. Add extra sea salt to taste.

WARNING: you will want to eat these straight out of the oven!

BELLA'S BEST SHEPHERD'S PIE

Family is very important to me – and that includes our four-legged friends. Being vegan is the best way to look after all beings and our planet. I am sharing this comfort food that both my wife, Moana, and Vinnie, who is central to our family, love.

SERVES 4–6

Mash

- 8 potatoes (I use Dutch Cream)
- 1 vegetable stock cube (optional)
- 120 g vegan butter
- ¾ cup plant-based milk (I use soy)
- ½ teaspoon salt

Filling

- 2 brown onions
- 2 carrots
- 4 stalks celery
- 6 cloves garlic
- 4 cups dried lentils or 2 x 400 g cans lentils
- 2–3 vegetable stock cubes
- 2–3 tablespoons olive oil
- 4 dates, pitted and chopped
- 2 bay leaves
- 1 bunch thyme, leaves only
- 2 stems rosemary, leaves only
- 2 tablespoons paprika
- 1 tablespoon cumin
- 5 tablespoons tomato paste
- 2 x 400 g cans diced tomatoes
- ⅓ cup currants
- 250 g silverbeet, stalks removed
- 150 g vegan cheese

Start cooking the potatoes for the mash while you make the filling.

FOR THE MASH, peel and cut the potatoes into quarters. Bring a large saucepan of salted water to the boil. Add potatoes and cook for 15–20 minutes or until soft. I like to put a vegetable stock cube in the water too.

Drain the cooked potatoes and add the butter, milk and salt to the saucepan and mash the potatoes till smooth. You might need more or less milk depending on the consistency of the mash. Put aside.

FOR THE FILLING, finely chop the onions, carrots, and celery. Grate the garlic. If cooking the lentils, bring a saucepan of salted water to the boil and add lentils. I like to put a vegetable stock cube in the water. Cook for 10–15 minutes or until tender. If using canned lentils, drain and rinse.

Heat the olive oil in a large saucepan. Add the onion and cook for a few minutes. Then add the garlic, carrot, celery, dates, bay leaves, thyme, rosemary, 2 vegetable stock cubes, paprika and cumin and cook for another 5 minutes until soft. Add the tomato paste and cook for another minute, then add the tomatoes and currants. Cook for 10 minutes.

Chop the silverbeet, add to the onion mixture and cook for another 5 minutes.

Add the lentils (cooked or canned) to the rest of the filling. If needed, add a little water. (I like to use a bit of the cooking water from the lentils.) Season with salt and pepper, to taste. Once the filling is cooked, transfer it to a baking dish. Remove the bay leaves. Top with mashed potato. Grate the vegan cheese and sprinkle over the top.

Put the oven on the grill setting at about 180°C. Grill the pie until the cheese has melted, which will take 7–10min.

'Being vegan
is a *great* way
to put compassion
into *action*.'

LEIGH-CHANTELLE

Recipe list

CONTINUED >

FEED *your family*

Nurture your loved ones *with* comfort food, curries *and* plenty of vegies

Recipe list continued

AUTHENTIC BUTTER 'CHICKEN' MASALA

POTATO *and* SPINACH CURRY

COMFORTING CHICKPEA CURRY

CAULIFLOWER, CASHEW *and* COCONUT CURRY

LENTIL *and* MUSHROOM CHUNKY CURRY

BUTTER BEANS *with* TIKKA MASALA SAUCE

CHICKPEA *and* SPINACH CURRY

LENTIL *and* QUINOA COCONUT CURRY

CRISPY SZECHUAN MUSHROOMS

PALAK PANEER

ROASTED GARAM MASALA BRUSSELS SPROUTS *with* COCONUT

EGGPLANT PARMY

WALKATOES (BAKED POTATOES *with* KALE *and* WALNUT SAUCE)

CREAMY MUSHROOM PASTA

It's not rocket science, but this makes a really lovely flavoured comfort dinner. Adding sage from the garden makes the classic garlic and mushroom combination even better. It's so good you'll want to eat any leftover mushroom sauce on toast for breakfast!

SERVES 3–4

Cashew cream

- 1 cup raw cashews
- 1 tablespoon nutritional yeast (optional)
- 1 clove garlic
- ½ teaspoon salt
- 1 packet of your preferred pasta

Sauce

- 1 brown onion, diced
- 4 cloves garlic, chopped
- 400 g mushrooms, sliced
- 1½ tablespoons olive oil
- 1 tablespoon fresh sage, finely chopped, plus 1 teaspoon extra
- cracked black pepper

FOR THE CASHEW CREAM, start by soaking the cashews overnight, or if you need them quickly, soak in boiling water for 20 minutes or so.

Rinse the soaked cashews and put them in a blender (or better still a high-powered thingy like a NutriBullet). Add 1½ cups water, the nutritional yeast, salt and garlic. Whizz it all up and then put it aside.

FOR THE PASTA, bring a large pot of salted water to a rapid boil, add pasta and cook according to packet instructions. Before draining, save a few ladles of the pasta water to add to the mushroom sauce if it becomes too thick.

FOR THE PASTA SAUCE, heat a large flat pan over low–medium heat. When heated, add the oil, then the onion and sauté, stirring, until the onions are soft and translucent but not browned (about 5 minutes).

Next add the chopped garlic and stir. Stop for a moment! Breathe in deeply. Reflect on your luck and continue stirring while the onion and garlic gently sizzle for about two minutes.

Add the tablespoon of sage. Stir – breathe it all in again – *mmm* – and stir for about a minute. Add the sliced mushrooms and stir they are softened and reduced – about 5 mins. Add cracked pepper and stir.

Add the cashew cream and stir. Season to taste with salt and pepper. Once the cream starts to bubble, turn the heat down to a mild simmer and cook for few minutes. Stir in some saved pasta water if the sauce is becoming a bit too thick.

Plate up the pasta, top with the sauce then sprinkle with the remaining chopped fresh sage.

RICH MUSHROOM *and* ASPARAGUS RISOTTO

This risotto is my new go-to when I'm trying to impress! I've always struggled to find a creamy vegan risotto that I loved, and this one is very rich and bursting with flavour. It isn't super simple, but the time it takes to cook is totally worth it. Hope you love it as much as I do!

SERVES 8

- 2.5 litres vegan stock (I use chicken-style)
- 40 g vegan butter (I use Nuttelex)
- ½ cup olive oil
- 2 brown onions, finely chopped
- 880 g arborio rice
- 1½ tablespoons fresh thyme leaves
- ½ cup dry white wine
- 200 g button mushrooms, sliced
- 100 g fresh shiitake mushrooms, sliced
- 1 handful of asparagus, cut into 2 cm pieces
- 4 cloves garlic, crushed
- salt and pepper

Bring the stock just to the boil in a large saucepan. Reduce heat and hold at a gentle simmer.

Heat the butter and 2 tablespoons of the oil in a heavy-based stockpot or large flameproof casserole over medium heat. Add the onion and cook, stirring, for 5 minutes or until soft and translucent but not coloured. Add the rice and 1 tablespoon of the thyme. Cook, stirring, for 1 minute or until the grains appear slightly glassy.

Add the wine to the rice mixture and cook, stirring, until the liquid is absorbed. Add a ladleful (about ½ cup) of the simmering stock to the rice and stir constantly with a wooden spoon until the liquid is absorbed. Continue adding the stock, a ladleful at a time, stirring constantly and allowing the liquid to be absorbed before adding the next ladleful, for 20–30 minutes or until the rice is tender yet firm to the bite and the risotto is creamy.

Heat the remaining oil in a large frying pan over high heat. Add the mushrooms, asparagus and garlic. Cook for 5 minutes or to your liking. Add to the risotto with the remaining thyme and stir well. Season with salt and pepper and serve.

NOTES Leftovers will keep in an airtight container in the fridge for about 2 days. ● To freeze, cool the risotto and transfer to an airtight container. Label, date and freeze for up to 3 months. Thaw in the fridge overnight.

TOFU GNOCCHI *with* PESTO *and* BLISTERED TOMATOES

Forget everything you know about making gnocchi – this recipe is easy! Unlike traditional potato gnocchi, there's no need to pre-cook anything. In next to no time you'll have soft little pillows of protein-enriched deliciousness.

SERVES 3

Lemon and basil pesto

- ¾ cup firmly packed basil leaves
- 2 tablespoons olive oil
- 2 tablespoons pine nuts
- 2 teaspoons lemon juice
- 1 small clove garlic, minced
- 2 teaspoons nutritional yeast
- generous pinch each of salt and cracked black pepper

Blistered tomatoes

- 200 g cherry tomatoes
- 1 tablespoon balsamic vinegar
- ½ tablespoon olive oil
- pinch each of salt and cracked black pepper

FOR THE PESTO, add all the ingredients to a food processor and blend until well combined but not completely smooth – leave a few small chunks for texture. You might need to scrape down the sides of the processor halfway through.

FOR THE TOMATOES, preheat the oven to 180°C.

Place all the ingredients into a small baking dish and toss to combine. Bake while preparing the gnocchi, until the tomatoes are starting to blister (about 15 minutes), stirring halfway through. Remove from the oven and set aside until ready to serve.

CONTINUED >

Tofu gnocchi

- 300 g silken tofu
- 1 cup plain flour, plus more for dusting
- 1 teaspoon arrowroot (tapioca flour) or cornflour
- ½ teaspoon salt
- ½ cup nutritional yeast
- pinch of white pepper

To serve

- 3 teaspoons pine nuts, toasted
- balsamic vinegar (optional)

FOR THE GNOCCHI, fill a large pot with water and bring to the boil on the stove.

Put all ingredients in a large bowl. Mash the tofu into the dry ingredients with a fork. Dust your hands with flour and then combine and press the mixture together to form a dough. The consistency should be very soft and a bit sticky (the softer the dough, the fluffier the gnocchi will be). Add some extra flour if it is too sticky to handle, and add a teaspoon of water at a time if it is too dry.

On a surface lightly dusted with flour, form the dough into a disc shape about 15 cm in diameter. Cut the disc into 8 wedges, dusting the blade of the knife with flour to prevent sticking. Roll each wedge into a long log shape, about 1.5 cm thick, and then cut into 3 cm lengths. Set gnocchi aside.

Add a generous pinch of salt to the pot of boiling water. Drop in the gnocchi, and once they're all in, stir the water once to prevent them sticking. Wait until the gnocchi rise to the surface (about 3 minutes). As each gnocchi starts rising to the top, remove it with a slotted spoon straight away. Drain any excess water from the gnocchi.

TO SERVE, mix the cooked gnocchi with the pesto. Spoon onto serving plates and top with the blistered tomatoes and pine nuts. If there's any marinade left over from the roasted tomatoes, drizzle it over the top of the gnocchi, or alternatively drizzle with balsamic vinegar.

NOTES The gnocchi is best eaten immediately after boiling as it will become firmer on standing. However, you can prepare the gnocchi ahead of time. Follow the process up until you've formed the log shape, then wrap each log separately in plastic wrap and store in an airtight container in the fridge for up to 2 days before cutting up and boiling. ● The gnocchi can also be served with any of your favourite pasta sauces, or with a store-bought pesto.

PAN-FRIED BEETROOT GNOCCHI *in* CREAMY MUSHROOM *and* SPINACH SAUCE

Not only are the gnocchi delicious and fluffy, they're also gluten-free! The colour theme at Good Love is pink, so it makes perfect sense to put lovely pink gnocchi on the menu. It was an instant hit! Choose potatoes that are good for mashing, like Dutch cream or Nicola.

SERVES 4–5

Almond feta

- 1 cup almond meal
- 1½ tablespoons extra virgin olive oil
- 2 tablespoons lemon juice
- ½ teaspoon sea salt

Gnocchi

- 550 g potatoes, peeled and chopped
- 65 g gluten-free flour mix
- 45 g chickpea flour
- pinch of sea salt
- 1 ¼ teaspoons beetroot powder

FOR THE ALMOND FETA, put all ingredients in a food processor with 25 mls water and blend for 30 seconds or until fully incorporated but still with a crumbly texture. Put the feta aside in a bowl.

FOR THE GNOCCHI, boil the potatoes in plenty of water until soft. Work it through a potato masher to get smooth mash. Let it cool down for a bit while you make the mushroom sauce.

To finish making the gnocchi, put the potato in a bowl with the flour mix, chickpea flour and salt. Knead it for 2–3 minutes until it has come together into a smooth soft dough. Don't over mix it. Add the beetroot powder and knead again until it's fully incorporated and has a nice pink colour.

On a floured bench, cut the dough in half and roll it out into a log, 2 cm in diameter, like a rope. Cut the dough into 2 cm pieces and put them aside

Mushroom sauce

- olive oil
- 1 brown onion, finely chopped
- 400 g button mushrooms, sliced
- 400 g king brown oyster mushrooms, sliced
- 3 tablespoons tomato paste
- 2–3 cloves garlic
- ½ tablespoon thyme leaves
- ½ teaspoon chilli flakes
- 1½ tablespoons maple syrup (or brown sugar)
- 3 tablespoons gluten-free tamari or soy sauce
- 1 teaspoon sea salt
- 1 tablespoons Massel vegan beef stock powder
- 1 x 400 ml can coconut cream
- 100 g enoki mushrooms
- 100 g spinach
- rocket, truffle oil and fried enoki (optional), to serve

FOR THE MUSHROOM SAUCE, heat some oil in a saucepan and cook the onions on medium heat till they're starting to soften, then add the mushrooms and cook until browned. Add the tomato paste, garlic, thyme, chilli flakes, maple syrup or sugar, tamari or soy sauce, and salt. Simmer for a couple of minutes. Add 2 cups water, stock powder and coconut cream, and let the sauce simmer for 15–20 minutes.

When the sauce is almost ready, start pan-frying the gnocchi in a bit of vegetable oil on low to medium heat until golden brown, about 5 minutes. Shake the pan so that the gnocchi are tossed around; be careful not to burn them. When the gnocchi are starting to get colour, add the enoki mushrooms. Fry for another minute. Then add the creamy mushroom sauce and the spinach. Toss around for another minute until everything is heated through completely.

Serve the gnocchi and the sauce in a bowl. Garnish with rocket and almond feta. Top it off with drops of truffle oil and some fried enoki (optional).

NOTES The gnocchi and the sauce will keep in airtight containers in the fridge for 4–5 days. Keep them in different containers for best results when reheating. • The gnocchi can be frozen either cooked or raw. Freeze the sauce in a separate container. Defrost overnight or in the microwave, and heat up in the pan for best results. • You can omit the beetroot powder if you can't find it easily. To make your own, mince up raw or cooked beetroot and dry it at 60°C for at least 10 hours in the oven or in a dehydrator. • Fried enoki are a delicious garnish for the gnocchi. In a deep fryer, fry 4 tiny bouquets of enoki for 2–3 minutes until golden brown.

LOUIS FOUNDLING | @ARLO_CAFE

ROASTED MUSHROOM, OLIVE, WALNUT *and* BROWN RICE RISOTTO

I'm sharing this beautiful healthy recipe because it's a family favourite of ours. It's packed full of nutrients and flavour, and it's a great winter warmer! What's more, this is no stand-by-the-stove risotto – you simply need to cook gently, stir occasionally and keep an eye on the vegies in the oven.

SERVES 4

- 500 g button mushrooms
- 100 g kalamata olives, pitted
- 100 g kale, leaves stripped from stems
- 4 cloves garlic
- 100 g walnuts
- salt and pepper
- 1 large brown onion, finely diced
- 2 cups brown rice
- 1 litre vegie stock
- 1 x 400 ml can coconut cream
- 1 small bunch dill, leaves chopped
- 1 lemon, juiced

Preheat the oven to 180°C.

Using whatever kitchen tools you have – hands included, my favourite kitchen tool! – to break up the mushrooms and olives, tear kale, slice garlic and crush the walnuts. Toss everything together with a good lug of olive oil, season with salt and pepper and spread on a large roasting tray. Roast for 20 minutes.

As soon as the tray is in the oven, it's risotto time!

Heat a little olive oil in a big pot with a lid over medium heat, and cook the onion gently until it's soft. Throw in the brown rice and stir for 1 minute.

Add all the stock and the coconut cream and season with a little salt and pepper. Stir and leave to simmer gently until the rice is soft enough to eat.

When the roasting vegies are looking good and the risotto liquid has been absorbed, combine everything in the big pot, along with the dill and lemon juice.

Finish with a drizzle of olive oil, divide between the plates, and . . . dinner is served!

NOTE The risotto will keep in an airtight container in the fridge for 3 days.

POTATO *and* ZUCCHINI GRATIN

I fell in love during quarantine lockdown (true story) and had a vivid lived experience of spending most evenings inventing dishes based on the abundant vegie box delivered each week. With all the global uncertainty and fear, it seemed important to focus on warm, salty comfort food to give our bellies a hug. I'm a carbohydrate and cheese fiend, so this combination of potatoes baked with the creamy alfredo sauce from Lauren Ulmer's *Vegan Yum Yum* cookbook was impossible to resist! PICTURED ON PAGE 100

SERVES 4

- 2 tablespoons olive oil
- 2 brown onions, thinly sliced
- 1 teaspoon brown sugar
- 3–4 gold potatoes, cut into thin 1.5 mm slices
- 3–5 zucchini, cut into 3 mm slices
- grated vegan cheese for topping (I use Vegusto No-Moo Piquant)
- salt
- side vegetables or salad, to serve

Sauce

- ⅓ cup raw cashews
- 1 cup plant-based milk (I use soy)
- ¼ cup nutritional yeast
- 3 tablespoons low-sodium tamari or soy sauce
- 2 tablespoons vegan margarine (I use Earth Balance)
- 1 tablespoon tahini
- 1 tablespoon lemon juice
- 2 teaspoons Dijon mustard
- ½ teaspoon paprika
- 1 pinch of nutmeg
- 2–4 cloves garlic, to taste
- black pepper

Preheat oven to 220°C.

Before you start making the gratin, soak the cashews (for the sauce) in boiling water for at least 30 minutes

Heat the oil in a cast iron frying pan (one you can use in the oven; alternatively you can transfer the mixture to a casserole dish when you're ready) on low–medium heat. Fry the onions for 10 minutes before adding the brown sugar and continue frying until they're caramelised and golden brown. Once the onions have cooled slightly, spread them evenly across the bottom of the frying pan and arrange the sliced potatoes and zucchini in concentric circles while you make the cheese sauce.

FOR THE SAUCE, blend all ingredients (including the soaked cashews) until smooth, then pour over the zucchini and potatoes. Top with grated cheese, then cover with foil.

Bake covered for 30–35 minutes or until the potatoes are tender when pierced with a fork. Remove the foil and bake for an additional 10 minutes to brown the top.

Top with extra salt if you're a salt maniac like myself, and serve warm, with salad or vegies. Prepare yourself for shrieks of delight from your fellow diners.

NOTE Leftovers will keep in an airtight container in the fridge for 3–5 days.

KURU FASULYE (TURKISH WHITE BEAN STEW)

There are cafes in Istanbul entirely dedicated to this traditional dish. When I first made this version, it brought tears to my eyes – I hadn't quite expected it to taste so good. The ingredients and the cooking method are simple enough, but brought together, the whole thing transcends the sum of the parts. PICTURED ON PAGE 100

SERVES 4

- 80 g mild–moderate fresh chillies
- approximately 400 g big tasty tomatoes, skinned and sliced thinly
- 4 tablespoons olive oil
- 1 large white onion, finely chopped
- 4 large cloves garlic, crushed
- 1 teaspoon chilli flakes
- 5 tablespoons tomato paste
- 120 g mushrooms, thinly sliced
- ½ red capsicum, thinly sliced
- ½ green capsicum, thinly sliced
- 2 teaspoons salt
- ½ teaspoon ground black pepper
- 500 g pre-cooked white beans (see note)
- plain rice pilaf and sumac, to serve

Preheat oven to 220°C.

Slice the chillies in half and place in a small roasting tin with 1 tablespoon olive oil. Cover with foil and roast for 40 mins. (Prepare the rest of the vegetables while the chillies are roasting.) Remove from oven and allow to cool a little. Place roasted chillies with roasting oil and up to 70 ml water in a blender and process until smooth. Set aside.

Heat 3 tablespoons olive oil in a big deep-sided pan, on medium–high heat. When hot, add onion and sauté for 3 minutes. Add garlic and chilli flakes, and sauté for 1 minute.

Add tomato paste and roasted chilli paste and sauté for 2 minutes. Add mushrooms and capsicums, and sauté for 1 minute. Add tomatoes and sauté for 1 minute. Add salt, black pepper and beans. Combine well.

Add just enough warm water to cover everything by about 1 cm and bring to the boil for a few minutes.

Reduce heat to minimum (use a heat diffuser if necessary) and cover. Cook for at least 40 minutes. It will simmer gently for about an hour.

Ten minutes before serving, taste and adjust seasoning if necessary.

Serve piping hot, with a plain rice pilaf, and sprinkled with sumac – a beautiful lemony-peppery traditional Middle Eastern spice.

NOTES Leftovers will keep in an airtight container in the fridge for a couple of days. • Dermason beans are perfect for this, but if you can't find them, cannellini beans are the next best thing. Using tinned beans is fine too.

ROAST PUMPKIN, SPINACH *and* TOFU LASAGNE

This tastes amazing and is great for when you're having friends over. It can be prepared in advance, and the leftovers make amazing lunches during the week. Nutritional yeast is like gold flakes for vegan cheesy meals. Have a chat to your health food shop and ask about ordering a big bag.

PICTURED ON PAGE 101

SERVES 4

- ½ jap pumpkin, peeled
- 60 g coconut oil
- 1 onion, finely chopped
- 2 cloves garlic, crushed
- 450 g firm tofu
- 250 g frozen spinach
- ¼ cup soy sauce
- 500 ml pasta sauce or passata
- 1 packet instant lasagne sheets
- salad of your choice, to serve

Cheese sauce

- 1 cup ground roasted cashews
- 1½ cups nutritional yeast
- pinch of sea salt
- 1 tablespoon flour
- 2 cups soy milk
- juice of half a lemon

Preheat oven to 180°C.

Cut the pumpkin into 1.5 cm thick wedges. Warm half the coconut oil and spread over a large baking tray and roast the pumpkin for 30 minutes, turning once.

While the pumpkin is roasting, start on the cheese sauce and the filling.

FOR THE CHEESE SAUCE, place cashews, nutritional yeast, salt and flour into a blender and blend until smooth. Bring the soy milk to the boil in a saucepan, reduce the heat and add the cashew mixture, whisking until smooth. Reduce to a simmer and cook for 5 minutes, stirring occasionally. Stir through lemon juice, remove from heat and leave to thicken.

FOR THE FILLING, heat remaining coconut oil in a pan. Add the onion and garlic and cook for 2 minutes. Add the tofu by crumbling small pieces into the pan. Add the frozen spinach and cook for 10 minutes, or until the spinach defrosts and mixes through the tofu. Add up to ¼ cup of water if the mixture starts to become dry. Add the soy sauce and cook for 2 minutes, then remove from heat.

TO ASSEMBLE THE LASAGNE, when the pumpkin is soft, start building the layers in a baking dish (mine is 20 cm x 30 cm) as follows:

1. a third of the pasta sauce followed by a layer of lasagne sheets, slightly overlapping
2. roast pumpkin, making sure the slices cover the sauce (like fitting jigsaw pieces together), topped with some of the cheese sauce, then a layer of lasagne sheets
3. tofu and spinach mixture, topped with a third of the pasta sauce, then a final layer of lasagne sheets
4. remaining pasta sauce and the rest of the cheese sauce.

Cover with foil and bake for 45 minutes, removing the foil after 25 minutes.

Remove from the oven and allow to cool for 5 minutes. Serve with a salad of your choice.

NOTES Leftover lasagne will keep in an airtight container for 4 days in fridge. • The cheese sauce can also be used for an easy mac and cheese with any pasta, or as a cauliflower and broccoli bake. Simply place broccoli and cauliflower pieces in a baking dish, cover with cheese sauce and bake for 30 minutes. • You can use gluten-free lasagne sheets, gluten-free flour and tamari sauce – ours is always gluten-free, and you would never know!

PREVIOUS PAGE (clockwise from top right):

Roast Pumpkin, Spinach and Tofu Lasagne
Roasted Cauliflower Tacos with Green Goddess Tahini Sauce, 108
Potato and Zucchini Gratin, 98
Kuru Fasulye (Turkish White Bean Stew), 99

AWESOME SPICY KIND *of* CHINESE STIR-FRY

So I like to keep things fairly simple in the kitchen. Get the vegetables how you want them, chuck them in the cooking device, add stuff to make it rule. That last bit is the important bit: the stuff to make it rule. I've been making tofu stir-fries for about 24 years, ever since I joined the band – Frenzal Rhomb – in the mid-nineties and got told to go vegetarian, and in that time I've learned the things that make it rule. You need the saltiness, the sweet stuff, and the spicy-as-hell stuff too.

SERVES 2

Tofu marinade

- 1 block firm tofu
- 3 tablespoons soy sauce
- 2 tablespoons sweet chilli sauce
- 2 teaspoons liquid smoke (we use Colgin Hickory, but they're all pretty much the same)

Before we start, there are two things you need to know. All amounts are approximate, because live your own life. And don't let anyone tell you that using packet or jar sauces is cheating!

FOR THE TOFU MARINADE, slice tofu block into 1 cm steaks. Press between two chopping boards lined with paper towel, with something heavy on top, for about 10 minutes (ideally prepare your tofu ages before your stir-fry, but it still tastes good if you do it while you're cutting up your vegetables).

Mix the soy sauce, sweet chilli sauce and liquid smoke in a bowl or plastic container. Press the tofu steaks into the marinade, coating both sides, and then stack them in a container or somewhere they can soak up the goodness. Chuck them in the fridge for a bit maybe.

CONTINUED >

Stir-fry

- 1 large onion
- 1 large carrot
- 1 head broccoli (I use all the broccoli, even the stems, because I'm an egalitarian)
- 1 Chinese broccoli (gai lan)
- 1 capsicum
- 1 large punnet pearl oyster mushrooms (see note)
- 1 bunch kale, with the harder stem bits cut off (I'm not that much of an egalitarian)
- half a bulb of garlic (yep, don't be a coward)
- bit of ginger
- oil (I use rice bran oil, but don't let me tell you what to do)
- 1 tablespoon vegetarian oyster sauce
- 1 tablespoon sweet chilli sauce
- 1 tablespoon soy sauce
- 1–2 tablespoons hot soybean paste (see note)
- jasmine rice and sliced spring onions, to serve

FOR THE STIR-FRY, cut up your vegies into the same shapes you see in your favourite Chinese takeaway. Break up the pearl mushrooms into individual little mushroom guys. Tear or chop the kales leaves. Crush the garlic and grate the ginger.

Heat up your electric wok to really very hot. If you don't have an electric wok, don't worry! Just go to the shops and buy one. Your life will be better. Pour in about 2 tablespoons of oil.

Add all the vegetables except the mushrooms and the leafy bits of the Chinese broccoli. Add the sauces and soybean paste. Add the mushrooms and Chinese broccoli tops, and mix everything in.

Taste it! We sometimes leave the garlic and ginger until last, to keep it tasting fresh, and sometimes salt and pepper are good.

While that's all happening, get a frying pan going on your stovetop, turn it up high and put your tofu steaks on it. Now fry the dickens out of them so they get a little charred with the sauces all caramelising. Turn them over and do the same to the other side.

Carefully transfer the tofu steaks from the frying pan to a chopping board, let them cool down enough to touch, then slice them into 5 mm strips, and in half lengthways too. Chuck those strips back in the frying pan with any leftover marinade. Stir them around a bit as they get all nice and crispy. Then, chuck the tofu strips into the wok with the stir-fry and give it all a good mix.

Serve it on top of the steamed jasmine rice you've quickly and easily prepared in your rice cooker. If you don't have one of those, you should have bought one when you went out to get an electric wok.

If you want, slice up some spring onions to go on top. Or don't. I'm not your mother.

NOTES About the hot soybean paste. The brand I use is from Taiwan and imported by Rockman, appropriately. I can't read the writing on the jar, but there's a donkey saying something, probably 'Man, this is hot'. Because it is! It's the secret ingredient, but you can't use too much, sadly, because it just makes everything too spicy. And I like it hot! ● Pearl oyster mushrooms are so delicious and perfect for this dish, but I hate having to buy the plastic punnets. So if you have a hook-up for these straight off the mushroom tree, please let me know!

CHIPOTLE JACKFRUIT TACOS

This is incredibly tasty thanks to the chipotle, and it looks fantastic on the plate! I've made it so many times, and everyone loves it. Depending on what you have in the fridge, you can keep it simple or really dress it up with extras when serving.

MAKES 8–10 TACOS

- oil, for frying
- 1 onion, sliced
- 4 cloves garlic, crushed
- 2 x 400 g cans jackfruit, drained
- ½ cup vegie stock or water
- juice of 1 lime (or more if you like it extra zesty)
- 1½ teaspoon ground chipotle
- 1 teaspoon ground cumin
- 1 teaspoon smoked paprika
- 1 teaspoon chilli powder (adjust to your liking)
- pinch of salt
- 8–10 tacos (I prefer corn for the authentic flavour)

To serve

avocado, red onion, coriander, pickled jalopenos or your favourite hot sauce

Heat the oil in a large pan over medium heat. Add the onion and sauté for about 5 minutes or until starting to brown. Add the garlic and sauté a further minute.

Tear the jackfruit into strips and add to the pan with the stock or water, lime juice and all the spices, season to taste, and cover. Reduce heat and simmer until the jackfruit starts to soften a little and the liquid is absorbed.

Mash the jackfruit slightly with a potato masher until you reach the desired texture – kind of like shredded pork.

Heat the tortillas in a pan according to the packet instructions.

Add the jackfruit filling, and anything you wish to serve it with: avocado, red onion, coriander, pickles or even your favourite hot sauce. Just remember: the chipotle is the star here and the flavour is incredible, so you may not need to add much to it!

NOTES Jackfruit filling will keep in an airtight container in the fridge for 3–5 days. It can also be frozen. • Use any pickled vegetable such as cabbage – this adds crunch, zest and colour to take your tacos to the next level!

ROASTED CAULIFLOWER TACOS *with* GREEN GODDESS TAHINI SAUCE

This is a super fresh, super versatile meal perfect for the whole family, packed full of goodness. Everyone will love the addictive green tahini sauce. We love tahini because it contains more protein than milk and most nuts. It's a rich source of B vitamins that boost energy and brain function; vitamin E, which is protective against heart disease and stroke; and important minerals such as magnesium, iron and calcium.

SERVES 4

Tahini sauce

- ⅓ cup tahini
- 1 cup fresh coriander leaves, plus more to serve
- ½ clove garlic
- juice of 1 lemon
- 1 teaspoon ground cumin
- ¾ teaspoon salt
- ¼ teaspoon black pepper

Tacos

- 1 medium cauliflower, chopped into florets
- 2 tablespoons olive oil
- 1 tablespoon cumin
- 1 tablespoon smoked paprika
- 1 teaspoon salt
- ½ teaspoon pepper
- 8 tortillas
- purple cabbage, shredded
- 1 avocado, sliced
- 1 chilli, sliced
- 1 lime, cut into wedges

Preheat oven to 180°C.

FOR TAHINI SAUCE, blend all ingredients in a small food processor or blender until the texture is similar to pesto. Gradually drizzle in 5 tablespoons water and blend until sauce is light green and creamy.

FOR TACOS, coat cauliflower with olive oil, cumin, paprika, salt and pepper. Roast for 25 minutes or until golden brown, tossing halfway through.

Heat tortillas according to packet instructions.

TO ASSEMBLE, fill each taco with roasted cauliflower. Top with the cabbage and sliced avocado, and drizzle with the tahini sauce. Garnish with extra coriander, chilli and lime. Margaritas optional!

NOTE Tahini sauce and roasted cauliflower can be stored in airtight containers in the fridge for up to 3 days. The tahini sauce can be frozen.

SPICY SWEET POTATO *and* MEXICAN BEAN ENCHILADAS

I especially love Mexican cuisine, and this dish is delicious, hearty, versatile and super easy to make. Cook the filling the day before so that you only need to quickly assemble and bake it on the day – brilliant for a gathering!

SERVES 4–8

- 1 small sweet potato
- 1 tablespoon vegetable oil
- 1 small red onion, finely diced
- 1 teaspoon chilli powder, or to taste
- 1 teaspoon garlic powder
- 1 tablespoon ground cumin
- 1 teaspoon dried oregano
- ½ teaspoon cayenne
- ½ cup short-grain brown rice, cooked and strained (or use pre-cooked rice)
- 1 cup canned kidney beans, washed well and drained
- 1 small red capsicum, diced
- ½ cup corn kernels, cooked
- 2 cups tomato puree
- salt and pepper
- 8 small wholemeal tortillas
- 1 x 375 g jar vegan-friendly enchilada sauce
- 1 cup shredded dairy-free cheese

To serve

blackened corncobs, avocado, steamed green beans, green salad

Preheat oven to 200°C.

Peeled and dice the sweet potato and steam until soft. Put aside.

Heat the oil in a large pan. Sauté the red onion on low heat until soft and slightly translucent.

Combine the chilli powder, garlic powder, cumin, oregano and cayenne. Add to the onion and cook for a minute or so.

Add the sweet potato, rice, kidney beans, capsicum, corn and tomato puree. Combine all the ingredients well, lightly crushing the sweet potato with the back of your stirring spoon.

Cook on low–medium heat for a couple of minutes. Stir occasionally so the mixture doesn't stick to the bottom of the pan. Check the seasoning and add salt and pepper to taste.

Lay the tortillas on the bench. Divide the mixture equally onto the middle of each tortilla, leaving space on the top, bottom and sides. Fold each side in till you have a parcel, and place on an oven tray. Top the enchiladas with your favourite mild enchilada sauce and the cheese.

Pop into the oven and cook until the enchiladas have started to colour and the cheese is melted.

Serve straight from the oven with all or some of: blackened corncobs, steamed green beans, avocado, a lovely crisp green salad ...

NOTES Leftovers will keep in the fridge in an airtight container for a couple of days, but no longer – cooked rice needs to be consumed in 1 to 2 days. The enchiladas can also be frozen.

ROASTED EGGPLANT *and* SAFFRON TOMATO SALSA

Eggplant is such a versatile yet complex ingredient, as this quick and easy recipe shows. Roasting the eggplant leaves it soft and silky smooth, ready to pair perfectly with the bright tomato flavours. It tastes great and looks lovely on the table as either a stand-alone dish or a vegetable side.

SERVES 6

- 1 kilo eggplant, cut into 1 cm slices
- 80 ml olive oil
- 100 g tomato paste
- 30–40 g lightly toasted pine nuts
- ½ cup chopped parsley
- pomegranate molasses (optional)
- brown rice, quinoa or roasted root vegetables, to serve

Salsa

- ½ teaspoon saffron threads
- 1 small red onion, diced
- 1 clove garlic, crushed
- small sprig rosemary, leaves chopped finely
- 1 teaspoon ground cumin
- ½ teaspoon smoked paprika
- splash of apple cider vinegar
- 400 g mixed or cherry tomatoes
- salt and pepper

Preheat oven to 200°C.

Brush eggplant slices with olive oil and tomato paste. Place in an ovenproof dish and roast for 20–30 minutes until cooked through.

FOR THE SALSA, soak saffron strands in 3–4 teaspoons water to soften, set aside.

In large frying pan, gently cook onion, garlic and rosemary on low heat, stirring until the onions are soft. Add cumin, paprika and apple cider vinegar along with the tomatoes.

Cover with a lid and simmer for 5–6 minutes until tomatoes have started to soften, then add the saffron and season to taste. The tomatoes should be a little warm and split, but not cooked to mush.

To assemble, create a base layer with half the eggplant and spoon over half the salsa. Create a 'stack' by using the remaining eggplant slices and salsa, then scatter with pine nuts and parsley. Optional magic – drizzle pomegranate molasses over the assembled dish for extra tang and brightness.

Serve warm as a main with brown rice, quinoa or roasted root vegetables or at room temperature as a salad.

NOTES Leftovers will keep in an airtight container in the fridge for a day. • As part of a larger meal, this goes with whatever you'd like to dish up alongside – a rocket and radicchio salad is awesome! • You can roast the eggplant and make the salsa the day before and store as separate components in the fridge. The salsa flavours will develop further overnight.

CREAMY VEGETABLE RAGOUT

A French-inspired dish with a Hungarian twist, this flavoursome and hearty stew is a favourite of mine. It's best served with some hot noodles tossed with fresh parsley, a little vegan butter, and some salt and pepper.

SERVES 6

- 1 teaspoon olive oil
- 1 onion, diced
- 2 cloves garlic, crushed
- 600–650 g washed potatoes, diced
- 375 g peeled carrots, diced
- 1 teaspoon chicken-style stock powder (I use Massel brand)
- 1 x 400 g can diced tomatoes
- 1 large red capsicum, finely chopped
- ½ teaspoon dried chilli flakes
- 1 tablespoon Hungarian paprika
- 1 tablespoon dried parsley
- 1 tablespoon dried thyme
- ½ teaspoon ground sage
- ⅓ cup pimiento-stuffed green olives, sliced
- 3 tablespoons capers
- noodles of your choice
- ⅓ cup vegan sour cream
- salt
- 1 teaspoon cracked pepper
- fresh parsley, to serve

Heat the oil in a pan. Sauté onion and garlic for a few minutes until onion has cooked.

Add the potatoes, carrots, stock powder, tomatoes and 2 cups water. Stir and then cover with frying pan lid. Cook over medium heat for 25–30 minutes, stirring occasionally.

Add the capsicum and all the herbs and spices. Continue to cook until the potatoes and carrot are tender, testing them with a skewer.

Add the olives and capers. Remove the lid and cook on low until the sauce thickens.

Cook the noodles according to packet instructions.

When the sauce has thickened and you're ready to eat, stir in the sour cream. Serve over hot noodles tossed with chopped fresh parsley, a little vegan butter and salt and pepper.

NOTES Leftovers will keep well in an airtight container in the fridge for 3 days. • Try making your own vegan sour cream using the recipes on pages 206 and 207.

ROBERT DEGUARA

MALTESE STUFFED EGGPLANT

Growing up in a Maltese family, all our meals revolved around meat. Try explaining to a Maltese mother or grandmother (nuna) that you don't eat meat anymore! When I turned vegan I missed some of the traditional meals Mum made. I adapted her Brungiel Mimli so my wife and I can enjoy them.

SERVES 4

- 6 large eggplant
- olive oil
- 1 onion, finely chopped
- 1 carrot, finely diced
- 1 zucchini, finely diced
- 1 tomato, finely chopped
- 1 mushroom, finely diced
- 400 g plant-based mince (I use Naturli)
- around 400 ml passata
- mixed Italian herbs
- fresh coriander
- breadcrumbs – lots!
- vegan parmesan
- roast potatoes and onions, steamed greens or salad, to serve

Preheat the oven to 180°C.

To prepare the eggplant 'sailing boats' (I'll explain later), cut the eggplants in half and steam them until the middle is soft. Mum used to bake them in the oven – either way works.

To make the filling, put a little olive oil in a large frying pan over medium heat. Add the onion and fry until golden. Fry the carrot, zucchini, tomato and mushroom until soft, then add the mince and break it all up until it is hard to distinguish from the other vegies.

Start slowly adding passata – you want to add enough so that it is like a pasta sauce, but without losing the mince consistency. (You might use less than 400 ml, you might use more.) Add the herbs and let it all simmer away for 20 minutes or so.

Back to the eggplant boats. Using a sharp knife, mark a 1 cm border of flesh all around the edge of the halved eggplant. Be careful not to cut all the way to the bottom. Using a spoon, dig out the flesh so that what's left looks like a sailing boat.

Line an oven tray with baking paper and lay the boats flesh side up.

Dice the eggplant flesh into 1 cm cubes, add these to the mince and mix it all together. Cook for another 5 minutes, then remove from heat. Spoon the mince and vegetable mixture into the eggplant sailing boats – really pack it in and then pile it up, like a hill.

Sprinkle breadcrumbs and vegan parmesan on top. I use lots of breadcrumbs! Drizzle with olive oil and bake until hot and the tops have browned – I sometimes cheat and grill the tops a little as well.

Mum always served these with roast potatoes and onions. You might want to add steamed greens or a salad. Enjoy!

AUTHENTIC BUTTER 'CHICKEN' MASALA

Butter chicken masala used to be a classic in our household, so when we turned vegan this was one of the first recipes I adapted.

PICTURED ON PAGE 122 (top)

SERVES 4

'Chicken' masala

- 300 g firm tofu or high-protein mock chicken
- 1 tablespoon garlic and ginger paste
- ½ teaspoon turmeric
- 1 teaspoon chilli powder
- 1 tablespoon oil
- 1 tablespoon yoghurt
- 1 tablespoon lemon juice

Curry

- 2 tablespoons cashews
- ½ teaspoon plus 2 tablespoon oil
- 1 teaspoon cumin seeds
- 1 medium onion, chopped
- 2 medium tomatoes, chopped
- 1 tablespoon garlic and ginger paste
- ½ teaspoon turmeric
- 2 teaspoons chilli powder (adjust to taste)
- 1 tablespoon ground coriander
- ½ teaspoon ground cumin
- 2 tablespoons sugar
- salt
- 2 tablespoons chopped coriander leaves
- rice or naan and dairy-free yoghurt, to serve

Pat dry the tofu or mock chicken. Mix with the rest of the masala ingredients and refrigerate for 30 minutes.

FOR THE CURRY, soak the cashews in ½ cup hot water for 10 minutes, then blend into a paste. Set aside.

Heat ½ teaspoon oil on medium heat in a medium-sized saucepan. Add cumin seeds and onion, and stir until lightly browned. Add tomatoes and keep stirring to avoid sticking. When the tomatoes are soft, remove from heat and cool for a bit before blending till smooth.

FOR THE 'CHICKEN' MASALA, lightly coat the inside of a saucepan in oil and fry the tofu or mock chicken pieces. Brown evenly on all sides and set aside.

In the same saucepan, heat 2 tablespoons oil and add the blended tomato mix. Add the ginger and garlic paste and mix for approximately 3 minutes. Keep stirring to avoid burning.

Add the spices and mix until the oil separates. (The oil has separated when you can see small bubbles of oil forming as a layer on top and at the peripheries of the curry paste. This can take 5–10 minutes.)

Add sugar and cook for 2 minutes, stirring. Add the cashew paste and continue to stir, gently simmering until well combined. Add a little water if the curry is too thick, or simmer longer to thicken further.

Once the curry is at the desired consistency, add the tofu or mock chicken. Cover and simmer on low heat for 5–10 minutes to allow the flavour to infuse the pieces. Keep stirring to avoid sticking and burning. Add salt to taste.

Transfer to a serving bowl and garnish with chopped coriander. Serve piping hot with rice or naan and dairy-free yoghurt on the side.

POTATO *and* SPINACH CURRY

After watching *Earthlings* [documentary], I went vegan overnight. I couldn't justify the treatment of animals by humans and I don't want any part of it. I'm very conscious of how we treat non-humans on our planet, and it's something I'm pretty passionate about. This recipe is my wife, Anna's – it's a family favourite!. **PICTURED ON PAGE 123 (far right)**

SERVES 4–6

- oil, for frying
- 1 onion, chopped
- ⅓ jar Patak's Korma Paste
- 1 x stock cube
- 1 x 700 g jar passata (or 2 x 400 g cans tomatoes, blended)
- 1 x 400 g can coconut milk
- 800 g–1 kilo potatoes (any kind), peeled and chopped into small cubes
- 250 g frozen spinach, chopped into cubes (or you can use fresh)
- 1 x 400 g can chickpeas, drained and rinsed (optional)
- basmati rice and pappadums, to serve

Heat a dash of oil in a large saucepan over medium heat and fry the onion for 5 minutes.

Add korma paste and stock cube and fry for a further 5 minutes.

Add passata and coconut milk and stir.

Add potatoes to the saucepan, followed by the frozen spinach.

Boil until the potato is cooked through (about 30 minutes, depending on how small you cut them).

Stir through chickpeas, if using.

Serve with basmati rice and pappadums – that's what we like best.

COMFORTING CHICKPEA CURRY

Working as a nurse on 12-hour shifts, it's very important to me to have a go-to dish that is easy to cook, can be prepared ahead of time, freezes well *and* nourishes my body. This curry is perfect! Not only is it very versatile in that it works with substituted ingredients, it provides all the nutritional components I need to get through day-to-day life.

PICTURED ON PAGE 123 (middle)

SERVES 5

- 1 teaspoon coconut oil
- 1 brown onion, diced
- thumb-size piece of ginger, peeled and finely grated
- 4 cloves garlic, minced
- 2 teaspoons curry powder
- 1 teaspoon dried coriander leaves
- 1 teaspoon sweet paprika
- 1 teaspoon cumin
- ½ teaspoon turmeric
- 1 head broccoli, florets cut in half, stalks diced
- 2 potatoes, peeled and diced
- ¼ butternut pumpkin, diced
- 200 g Swiss brown mushrooms, sliced
- a few slices of eggplant, diced
- half a lemon, juiced
- 2 x cups cooked chickpeas
- 2 x 400 ml cans coconut milk
- 2 ½ cups chopped tomatoes
- salt and pepper
- rice, lemon, coconut yoghurt and fresh coriander, to serve

Heat the coconut oil in a pan over medium heat and sauté the onion until translucent. Add the ginger and garlic, and sauté for 2 minutes.

Add all the spices along with 3 teaspoons water and sauté until fragrant.

Add broccoli stalks, potatoes, pumpkin, mushrooms, eggplant and lemon juice. Cook for 5 minutes.

Add chickpeas, coconut milk and tomatoes. Bring to the boil, then simmer uncovered for 40 minutes.

Add broccoli florets and simmer for another 5 minutes. Season to taste.

Serve on a bed of your favourite rice with a squeeze of fresh lemon, a dollop of coconut yoghurt and some fresh coriander.

NOTE This curry keeps in an airtight container for 3–4 days in the fridge. It can also be frozen.

CAULIFLOWER, CASHEW *and* COCONUT CURRY

This was one of the first true vegan recipes I found following my transition from vegetarian to vegan, and over time I've perfected it. It can be cooked in advance and frozen, which makes it perfect for our busy household.

PICTURED ON PAGE 122 (bottom)

SERVES 4–6

Spice mix

- 1 tablespoon ground cumin
- 1 tablespoon ground coriander
- 2 teaspoons yellow mustard seeds
- 1 teaspoon ground turmeric
- ½ teaspoon garam masala
- ½ teaspoon fennel seeds, crushed
- 6 curry leaves, finely chopped
- pinch of cinnamon
- ½ teaspoon pink salt
- pinch of black pepper

Curry

- 2 tablespoons olive oil
- 1 large onion, chopped
- 2 cloves garlic, finely chopped
- 1 small piece ginger
- 2 small red chillies, finely chopped
- 1 x 400 ml can coconut milk
- 1 cup chicken-style stock
- 1 large cauliflower, cut into florets
- 1 cup raw cashews
- ½ cup sultanas, soaked in boiling water for 10 minutes until plump
- ½ cup coconut flakes, toasted
- steamed rice, dried chilli flakes and fresh coriander, to serve

For the spice mix, combine everything in a small bowl.

Peel and finely chop the ginger.

Pour olive oil in a saucepan or stovetop casserole dish, and warm on low heat. Sauté the onion until translucent, then add the garlic and ginger and gently cook for a few minutes. Add the spice mix and chillies and cook for a further minute.

Add the coconut milk and stock, stirring well to ensure the bottom of the saucepan is not sticking. Add cauliflower florets, stir to combine and bring to the boil.

Turn heat to low, cover and cook for 15 minutes. Remove lid, add cashews and cook for a further 10 minutes. Add sultanas and cook for another 5 minutes or until cauliflower is soft and tender.

Top with coconut flakes, dried chilli flakes and fresh coriander.

Serve with steamed rice.

NOTES Leftover curry keeps in an airtight container in the fridge for 3–4 days, and can be frozen. • When cauliflower is in season, it is also a great budget-friendly meal.

FOLLOWING PAGE (clockwise from top left):

Authentic Butter 'Chicken' Masala, 118
Comforting Chickpea Curry, 120
Potato and Spinach Curry, 119
Cauliflower, Cashew and Coconut Curry

LENTIL *and* MUSHROOM CHUNKY CURRY

This hearty aromatic curry is built around a mushroom product that gives the oomph that great comfort food needs. Get creative and use this as a filling for a piping hot crusty family-size pie. (PS, leftovers are great in a toastie.)

SERVES 6

- 1 cup dried green lentils
- 1–2 vegan stock cubes
- 2 teaspoons mustard seeds
- 2 teaspoons cumin seeds
- 2 teaspoons coriander seeds
- 1 teaspoon ground turmeric
- 1 teaspoon curry powder
- 1 teaspoon garam masala
- 2 tablespoons (or thereabouts) olive oil
- 1 onion, finely chopped
- 3–4 cloves garlic (to taste), crushed
- 300 g Lamyong Mushroom Chunks or Nuggets, defrosted (see note)
- 1 x 400 g can cherry tomatoes
- 3 large or 6 medium mushrooms, diced
- 100 ml coconut cream
- rice or mashed potato, green vegetables, to serve

Place the lentils, 2 cups water and stock cubes into a saucepan and bring to the boil. Simmer for approximately 20 minutes, until cooked but not overly soft (they should retain their shape). Add a little more water if needed, but do not make it too runny. Set aside.

Halve the mushroom chunks. Set aside.

Use a mortar and pestle to grind the mustard seeds, cumin seeds and coriander seeds. Add the turmeric, curry powder and garam masala to the mortar and mix. Set aside.

Now for the cooking bit! Heat the olive oil in a large heavy-based pan (wide and shallow is best) on medium heat, then add the onions and garlic and allow to soften (a few minutes).

Add the spice mix to the saucepan. Stir for several minutes to coat the onion and garlic and bring out the flavour of the spices (don't burn them).

Add the mushroom chunks to the saucepan and stir constantly so they are coated. Add a little more oil if needed. Move the chunks around for a few minutes to add a little colour.

Now add the rest: the lentils, tomatoes and fresh mushrooms. Bring to the boil, reduce heat and simmer for around 15 minutes. Add the coconut cream, stir and allow to rest for 10 minutes prior to serving.

Serve with rice or mashed potato and some green vegetables.

NOTES Leftovers keep well in an airtight container in the fridge for 3–4 days ● Double the recipe and freeze half for the next cold winter's night. ● The chunks (main ingredient: shiitake mushrooms) are available from the Cruelty Free Shop. ● Use any type of soy-based chunks to attain a similar consistency.

BUTTER BEANS *with* TIKKA MASALA SAUCE

This is a very versatile sauce, based on a recipe from veganricha.com – a great source of inspiration for vegan dishes. I've added butter beans for a hearty, easy-to-prepare dish, but you could go with roasted potatoes, beans, sweet potato, cauliflower, vegan sausages ... the possibilities are endless. This is quite a hot sauce, so reduce the spice quantities as needed.

SERVES 3–4

- 1 tablespoon oil
- 1 large onion, chopped
- 1 green chilli, chopped
- 1 teaspoon Himalayan salt
- 1 teaspoon ground ginger
- 1 teaspoon garlic powder
- 1 large tomato, chopped
- 1 teaspoon ground turmeric
- 1 teaspoon garam masala
- 1 teaspoon paprika (or smoked paprika)
- ½ teaspoon ground coriander
- ½ teaspoon chilli powder
- 1 x 400 g can tomatoes
- ½ cup non-dairy yoghurt
- 1 x 400 g can butter beans
- rice and vegies, to serve

Heat the oil in a pan on medium heat and sauté the onion until translucent, about 3 minutes. Add the chilli and stir.

Reduce the heat and add in salt, ginger and garlic powder. Stir for 2 minutes.

Add chopped tomato. Stir for another minute, then add the remaining spices and mix well.

Add canned tomatoes and stir for a further minute.

Add non-dairy yoghurt and mix well.

Add butter beans, reduce heat and let simmer for 30 minutes.

Serve on a bed of rice with a side of vegies.

NOTES Leftovers keep in an airtight container in the fridge for 3–4 days. The sauce freezes well. ● Wattie's Mexican-style tomatoes (available in New Zealand) are great in this dish.

CHICKPEA *and* SPINACH CURRY

Bright, fragrant and packed full of goodness, cooler weather is the perfect time to serve this aromatic curry. With protein from chickpeas, spinach and capsicum providing essential vitamins and minerals, and anti-inflammatory benefits from turmeric and cumin, this dish not only tastes amazing, it's incredibly healthy as well.

SERVES 2

- olive oil or coconut oil, for frying
- ½ onion, finely diced
- 3 cloves garlic, minced
- 2 teaspoon ground cumin
- 2 teaspoon ground turmeric
- ½ teaspoon cracked black pepper
- 2 tablespoons red curry paste
- 1 red capsicum, chopped
- 1 x 400 g can chopped tomatoes
- 1 tablespoon tomato puree
- 300 ml vegetable stock
- 1 x 400 g can chickpeas, drained and rinsed
- pinch of cayenne
- large handful of spinach, stalks removed
- brown rice or naan bread, to serve

Heat a drizzle of the oil in a large frying pan on medium heat and sauté the onion until soft, about 5 minutes.

Add the garlic, cumin, turmeric, pepper and curry paste and sauté until fragrant, about 2 minutes.

Add the capsicum, tomatoes, puree and stock. Bring to the boil, then lower the heat and add the chickpeas and cayenne. Simmer for 20 minutes

Roughly tear the spinach leaves and stir into the curry. Allow spinach to wilt, then remove the curry from the heat.

Serve over brown rice or with naan bread.

NOTE Leftover curry keeps in an airtight container in the fridge for 3 days. It can also be frozen.

LENTIL *and* QUINOA COCONUT CURRY

This is such a warming, hearty and nourishing meal to enjoy anytime. I get many compliments whenever I serve this dish. It's also very versatile – feel free to play around with the vegetables. For example, use spinach or silverbeet instead of kale. Enjoy!

SERVES 2

- 1 tablespoon olive oil (or coconut oil)
- 1 onion, finely diced
- 1–2 carrots, cut into large dice
- 1 red capsicum, cut into large dice
- 1–2 teaspoons crushed garlic
- 1 tablespoon finely grated ginger
- 1 tablespoon gochujang paste (or any spicy vegan curry paste)
- ½ teaspoon turmeric
- 1 teaspoon curry powder
- 500 ml vegetable stock or water
- 1 x 250 ml can light coconut milk
- 1 tablespoon tamari
- 100 g quinoa, white or red
- 100 g red lentils
- 2 cups kale, spine removed and leaves roughly chopped
- 1 tablespoon lime juice
- 15 g fresh coriander and basil, chopped
- chopped chillies, chopped chillies, coconut kefir, coriander sprigs, lime and naan bread, to serve

Heat the oil in a heavy-based saucepan on medium heat. When hot, add the onion, carrots and capsicum, and cook for 3–4 minutes.

Next, stir in the garlic, ginger, gochujang, spices and cook for another 2–3 minutes until fragrant.

Stir in the stock, coconut milk and tamari and bring to the boil. Add the quinoa and lentils stirring to combine.

Reduce the heat to a simmer, cover with a lid and cook for a further 25 minutes, stirring occasionally.

Add the kale and cook for a further 5 minutes, uncovered.

Remove from the heat, add the lime juice and fresh herbs, and stir to combine.

Ladle the curry into warmed bowls, and top with chopped chillies and a dollop of kefir. Garnish with coriander sprigs and lime, and serve with warm naan bread on the side.

NOTE Leftovers will keep in an airtight container in the fridge for 3–4 days. It can also be frozen.

CRISPY SZECHUAN MUSHROOMS

When my husband and I went out for dinner and he ordered beef Szechuan, I was inspired to make my own vegan version. After a little experimentation it is so amazing that it's now a family favourite. The recipe has a few steps but is truly worth the effort.

SERVES 4

300–400 g oyster or pearl mushrooms, cut into medium size pieces

Marinade

- 3 cups vegan red wine
- 2 cups soy sauce
- 1 cup brown sugar
- 4 sprigs rosemary, chopped roughly
- 4–5 cm piece ginger
- 2 teaspoons garlic, minced

Szechuan pepper sauce

- 2 cups vegan hoisin sauce
- 2 cups vegan mushroom oyster sauce
- ½ cup caster sugar
- 2 teaspoons ground or minced ginger
- 2 tablespoons ground Szechuan peppercorns, toasted

Tempura batter

- ½ cup cornflour
- ½ cup plain flour, sifted

To serve

- steamed rice or vegan fried rice
- 2 spring onions, sliced
- ¼ cup sesame seeds, toasted
- sliced red chilli

FOR THE MARINADE, mix all ingredients together. Place mushrooms in a non-metallic dish and pour over marinade. Refrigerate for 8–10 hours or up to 2 days.

FOR THE SZECHUAN PEPPER SAUCE, add all sauce ingredients to a saucepan and heat through until sugar has dissolved. Keep warm until ready to serve.

FOR TEMPURA BATTER, whisk ingredients together with 1 cup iced water to form a thin batter.

Have deep-fryer or wok with vegetable oil ready on 180°C. Drain marinade from mushrooms and reserve for another time.

Dip the mushrooms in the tempura batter, a quarter of the pieces at a time.

Deep-fry until crispy, then drain on paper towel and keep warm in oven while you batter and fry the remaining pieces.

To serve, either mix fried mushrooms with sauce or serve sauce separately. The first time I made this we mixed it all together, and it looked amazing and tasted great, but now we add the sauce at the table so everyone can have as much as they like. It's quite sweet, so a little bit goes a long way.

Serve with either steamed rice or vegan fried rice. Garnish with spring onions, toasted sesame seeds and sliced red chilli.

NOTES Mushrooms are best eaten on the day as the batter goes soggy in the fridge, but they can be reheated in the oven until crispy. Leftover sauce will keep in an airtight container in the fridge for up to 2 weeks.

PALAK PANEER

My first taste of palak paneer was over 20 years ago on an extremely cold overnight bus ride from Delhi to Dharamsala. We stopped at some roadside stands, where I spotted the jewel-like bright green of this dish and knew it was vegetarian. It was so delicious! I've used tofu instead of paneer (a soft Indian cheese), since tofu is similar in consistency.

SERVES 4

- 3 cups (packed) washed spinach leaves or 500 g frozen spinach, thawed
- 2 cm piece of fresh ginger, chopped
- oil of your choice, for frying
- 350 g firm tofu, cut into 2 cm cubes
- ¼ teaspoon chilli powder
- ½ teaspoon chilli flakes, or one fresh chilli
- 1 teaspoon cumin seeds
- 1 onion, finely chopped
- 4 cloves garlic, finely chopped
- 2 tomatoes, finely chopped
- ½ teaspoon turmeric
- ½ teaspoon salt
- ½ teaspoon garam masala
- rice, naan or pappadums, to serve

Blanch the fresh or frozen spinach in a pot of lightly salted boiling water for a couple of minutes. Drain and rinse in cold water to halt the cooking.

In a food processor, blend the drained spinach with the ginger and about ¼ cup of water. (Tip: use water saved from the drained spinach for extra nutrients.) Blend until fine and creamy in consistency. Add more water if necessary.

Heat a tablespoon of oil in a large pan on medium heat. Lightly fry the tofu cubes until just starting to turn golden. Remove, drain on paper towel and put to one side.

Turn the heat to medium–low and cook the chilli and cumin seeds for about 45 seconds, adding a little more oil if necessary.

Add the onion and garlic and sauté for about 8 minutes until the onion is soft.

Add the tomato and cook until soft, about 5–10 minutes.

Add the spinach puree, the turmeric and salt. Stir to combine well. Add up to ¼ cup water and simmer on medium–low heat for 5 minutes. Taste and add extra chilli or salt, if needed.

Add the tofu and garam masala, stir and simmer for 5 more minutes.

Serve with rice, naan or pappadums.

NOTES Palak paneer will keep in an airtight container in the fridge for up to 5 days. It also freezes well – thaw to room temperature and then reheat. ● The spinach can be replaced by other leafy greens.

ROASTED GARAM MASALA BRUSSELS SPROUTS *with* COCONUT

These brussels sprouts are rubbed with garam masala and coconut oil, then roasted with chewy coconut until they are slightly sweet. This dish immediately and deliciously cancels out any recent carb-loaded debauchery!

SERVES 2–4

- 600 g brussels sprouts, washed and patted dry
- ½ cup shaved coconut
- 4 tablespoons coconut oil, melted
- 3 teaspoons garam masala
- ¼–½ teaspoon chilli powder (optional)
- 1 teaspoon cumin seeds
- ¾ teaspoon salt
- half a lime
- non-dairy yoghurt, to serve

Preheat the oven to 200°C.

Discard the stems off the brussels sprouts and cut them in half lengthwise.

In a large roasting pan, toss all the ingredients using your (clean) hands, rubbing the spices into the cut surfaces of the sprouts.

Roast for 35–45 minutes, tossing in the pan every 10 minutes or so until the sprouts are crisp-edged, tender inside, but still holding together and a little chewy.

Squeeze lime juice generously over the sprouts before serving.

Serve as a side, or a light meal with a dollop of vegan yoghurt on top.

NOTES Leftovers will keep in an airtight container in the fridge for 2–3 days. Pan fry to reheat. ● Use shredded coconut if you can't find shaved coconut.

EGGPLANT PARMY

Here's my wife @audreygriffen's vegan, gluten-free eggplant parmy. It's the tastiest. No amounts here, you'll just need to eyeball it. I've quoted her directly where it's important.

SERVES 2

- eggplant, cut in 1 cm slices, lengthwise
- salt
- gluten-free plain flour
- cornflour (or tapioca flour)
- soy milk, to make the 'wash'
- gluten-free breadcrumbs (Aldi does good ones)
- dried herbs (optional)
- olive oil, for frying
- vegan cheese slices
- nutritional yeast flakes
- parsley, to serve

Sauce

- 1 x 680 g jar passata
- garlic powder
- Italian mixed herbs

How do you make the sauce, honey? 'Chuck it all together and cook it down.' (Reduce it.)

What about the eggplant? 'Generously salt it, and leave it to dry out for about 20–30 minutes.'

Use paper towel to dab it dry afterwards.

'Remember to turn the oven on to heat up.'

What temperature? '180 degrees.'

Use the cornflour to thicken the soy milk to make the 'wash'.

Next, you'll need to set up three bowls:

1. gluten-free flour with a pinch of salt
2. soy milk and cornflour wash
3. gluten-free breadcrumbs. Add a pinch of dried herbs to the breadcrumbs if you like.

Moving from one bowl to the next, cover the eggplant in flour, then dip in the wash, then the breadcrumbs.

Heat a bit of oil in a frying pan on a decent medium–high heat.

How long do I fry the eggplant for? 'Until there's colour on the crumb.'

When they're done, put the slices on paper towel to absorb excess oil, then place on a baking tray and pour the sauce over the eggplant.

Spread the vegan cheese slices on top, then sprinkle with nutritional yeast flakes.

How long do I cook it for? 'Whack it in the oven for about 20 minutes until it's nice and squishy.'

Maybe add some chopped parsley. Eat it!

WALKATOES (BAKED POTATOES *with* KALE *and* WALNUT SAUCE)

Walkatoes might sound a bit silly, but then walnut, potato and kale doesn't sound exciting enough for this delicious dish. This is so easy (especially if you have leftover baked potatoes), and I can't stop eating it. The creamy and slightly sour sauce combines so well with the leafy kale, and the baked potatoes provide a warm and satisfying base for this delightful combination of flavours.

SERVES 4

- 6–8 medium potatoes
- 1 bunch kale
- 1 clove garlic, unpeeled
- 1 cup walnuts
- juice of 1 lemon
- 1 tablespoon soy sauce
- a few walnuts, to serve

Preheat the oven to 180°C.

Wash and peel the potatoes and cut into quarters. Place on a tray lined with baking paper, and bake in the oven for around 40 minutes, or until golden on the outside and soft in the middle. At the 30-minute mark, add the clove of garlic.

Wash the kale, strip the leaves from the stem and tear into pieces. Bring a saucepan of water to the boil, then cook the kale for 3–5 minutes or until leaves are softened. Drain.

For the walnut sauce, put the walnuts, ¾ cup water, lemon juice, soy sauce and the baked clove of garlic (peeled) in a blender, and whiz until smooth.

Mix together the kale and walnut sauce, making sure every leaf is covered. To serve, put the potatoes in a bowl, top with the kale mix and sprinkle with a few walnuts if you wish.

NOTES Leftovers keep well in an airtight container in the fridge for 3 days. ● Replace lemon juice with lime juice or ½ tablespoon balsamic vinegar to vary the flavour.

'I respect *all* animals for *who* they are – *Living, feeling beings.*'

KERRY CHAPLIN

Recipe list

POTLUCK

Share a plate
with your mates

THE CHEESY CARBSTRONG BAKE

This is an easy-to-prepare healthy vegan meal that is so delicious I make it at least three times a week. Remember, the best way to help animals is to vote with your fork and choose a plant-based diet.

SERVES 3–4 (OR 2 HUNGRY VEGANS)

- 300g wholemeal penne pasta
- oil
- 300g broccoli, chopped
- 1 small onion, diced
- 1 teaspoon garlic, minced
- 1 x 400 g can chopped tomatoes
- 250 g unsweetened vegan yoghurt (I use Alpro Plain)
- 1 vegan stock cube
- herbs of your choice (mixed herbs are good)
- 40 g nutritional yeast
- 100 g grated vegan cheese (I use vegan mozzarella)
- 150 g plant-based protein of choice (tofu, seitan, tempeh, legumes or plant-based meat)
- fresh green salad, to serve

Before you start, get your kitchen tools ready. You'll need a big pasta pot and strainer, a saucepan, a decent-sized lasagne dish, a knife, a chopping board and a wooden spoon.

Pre-heat oven to 220°C.

First, get some water boiling for the pasta. Then add your pasta to cook while you make the sauce. Check packet instructions for how long to cook it.

Heat a little oil in a saucepan and sauté your onions and garlic until the onions have softened. Then add your chosen plant-based protein. Once that's cooked, add the chopped tomatoes, stock and herbs to taste.

When your pasta is about halfway there, add the broccoli so they can cook together.

Continue cooking the sauce until it is thick and fragrant. Put the sauce to one side to cool down for a few minutes, then add the yoghurt and three quarters of the nutritional yeast and stir to combine.

Once the pasta and broccoli are cooked, strain the water out and put them back into the pot you boiled them in.

Add the sauce to the pasta and broccoli and stir until completely combined. Place the whole lot evenly into the lasagne dish.

Sprinkle over the mozzarella so that it is evenly coated and sprinkle the remaining nutritional yeast over the top. Place in the oven and bake until the top is golden brown.

Dish it up with a green salad on the side. Enjoy!

NOTE Leftovers will keep in an airtight container in the fridge for 3 days. It also freezes well.

HIAM'S FALAFEL *with* TAHINI

This is a vegan dish we have at our shop. It's my mamma's recipe, and it's the most amazing falafel I've ever eaten. It has a beautiful green herby flavour, and is so good for you, too! We both play around with the mix of herbs according to the season. Mamma uses a hand mincer and we use a high-powered blender. You'll work out what ratio of chickpeas to herbs gives the perfect texture in your blender, and what suits your taste. Give it a go!

MAKES 24–28 BALLS

- 2–2½ cups dried chickpeas
- 2–3 cloves garlic, chopped finely
- ½ cup chopped flat-leaf parsley
- ¼ cup chopped mint
- ¼ cup chopped coriander
- sunflower oil, for shallow frying
- ½ teaspoon bicarbonate of soda
- sesame seeds, for rolling
- ⅓–½ cup tahini
- juice of 1 lemon
- salt

To serve

- Lebanese or pita bread
- salad fillings such as tomato, lettuce, cucumber, pickled turnip

Soaked the chickpeas for 24 hours, changing the water 2 or 3 times.

Drain the soaked chickpeas, and blend with garlic and herbs until a thick paste is formed. Add bicarb soda and 100 ml water, and blend.

Form into walnut-sized balls. Roll in sesame seeds, cover and let sit for 30 minutes.

Heat oil in a pan on medium heat, and when hot, shallow-fry the balls until golden brown on all sides. Cook them 'hot and fast'.

Meanwhile, whisk tahini, lemon juice and salt to taste.

To serve, slightly squash 2 or 3 balls and wrap in Lebanese or pita bread along with a drizzle of tahini sauce and salad fillings to taste.

NOTE Falafel balls will keep in an airtight container in the fridge for 3–4 days. ● The falafel mixture can also be frozen, before or after rolling into balls.

EASY ROASTED VEGETABLES *with* CAPERS *and* LEMON

This crowd pleaser is delicious warm as a side dish with lunch or dinner. It's also really good as a cold salad the next day.

SERVES 6–8

- 1 whole cauliflower
- 1 head of broccoli
- salt and pepper
- 1–2 tablespoons mixed herbs or marjoram
- extra virgin olive oil
- 3 tablespoons capers, drained and chopped
- juice of 1 or 2 lemons

Preheat oven to 180°C.

Remove outer green leaves from the cauliflower. Cut off the end of the stem so that the cauliflower can stand upright.

Cut the cauliflower head into 1cm slices. Some pieces will stay on the root, that's fine.

Do the same with the broccoli.

Spread the vegetables in a baking dish and season with salt and pepper. Sprinkle with 1 tablespoon of the herbs and drizzle well with olive oil.

Roast in the oven until the edges of the vegies are brown, turning once during the roasting time. This will take 30–40 minutes.

While the vegies are roasting, make a dressing by combining the capers, lemon juice, remaining herbs and 2 tablespoons olive oil. Mix well.

Once the vegies look nice and brown around the edges, remove from the oven and let stand for 5 minutes.

Drizzle with the caper dressing, season with salt and pepper and serve.

NOTE Leftovers make a great salad. Just add lettuce, sliced roma tomatoes, some sliced spring onion and a little more dressing.

SMOKY ADZUKI BEAN TEMPEH *with* ROASTED CAULIFLOWER

For my wife, @LisaLuckiest and I, being vegan means we can live healthier and longer lives and be there for our kids, do our bit for the environment and protect animals from cruelty. For us, meal times are about eating more vegetables, and cauliflower is the star here, taking on the smoky flavours of the tomato sauce. Tempeh is a great source of protein. We love this: it's easy to prepare and ticks all our boxes. PICTURED ON PAGE 145

SERVES 2

- olive oil, for frying
- 2 onions, chopped
- 2 cloves garlic, minced
- 2 x 400 g cans tomatoes
- salt and pepper
- 2 chipotles in adobo
- 1 small cauliflower
- 1 x 300 g packet tempeh, cut in 1 cm cubes

To serve

- 1 avocado, sliced
- fresh coriander leaves
- 1 lime, cut into wedges

Preheat oven to 200°C.

Heat a little oil in a saucepan over a medium–low heat, and soften the onions and garlic. It should take 8–10 minutes, but you can tell the onions are ready when they smell sweet.

Add the tomatoes. Turn up the heat and keep at a simmer for 3 minutes. Season generously with salt and pepper.

Add the chipotle chillies and a generous spoonful of adobo sauce. Heat for another 3 minutes to allow the flavours to combine.

Remove from the heat, and leave to cool a little while.

Cut the cauliflower into florets. Toss in oil and spread out on a baking sheet. Roast at the top shelf of the oven at for about 20 minutes.

Process the tomato mixture with a stick blender until smooth.

Heat some oil in a large frying pan and brown the cubed tempeh on each side. This is not a quick process – it might take 12 minutes.

Once the tempeh is browned, add the sauce. The tempeh might break apart slightly, but that's no problem – it's all delicious!

Serve the cauliflower in bowls with the tempeh and sauce, and top it all with sliced avocado, chopped coriander and lime wedges.

NOTES Tempeh is traditionally made with soybeans, but it can be made with just about any beans. ● If you can't find adzuki bean tempeh, use whatever variety is available at your local supermarket or Asian grocery.

CRUNCHY BLACK RICE SALAD

I want to preface this recipe by saying *please* don't ever be put off by a longish list of ingredients! It's often the recipes with greatest number of ingredients that are the easiest, require the least amount of skill, and are the quickest to make. This is such an easy recipe. If you haven't cooked with black rice before, absolutely give it a try. Its firm, nutty texture is bold, and it's packed full of nutrients. **PICTURED ON PAGE 145**

SERVES 6–8

½ cup black rice (see Notes)
1 tablespoon vegetable oil
1 small brown onion, finely diced
10 button mushrooms, sliced
pinch of salt and pepper
2 large silverbeet leaves, stems removed, leaves roughly chopped
3 tablespoons coriander stems, finely sliced
large handful of basil leaves, chopped

Dressing

1 tablespoon soy sauce
2–3 drops sesame oil
½ tablespoon freshly squeezed lime juice
½ teaspoon minced ginger
1 large clove garlic, minced
1 small red chilli, seeds removed, very finely diced
1 teaspoon maple syrup

To serve

½ cup of roasted, unsalted peanuts
½ cup of Chang's fried noodles
extra sliced chilli (optional)

Cook the rice according to packet instructions – black rice can have different cooking times.

Place all the dressing ingredients in a small bowl. Set aside.

While the rice is cooking, heat the oil in a medium pan and cook the onion on gentle heat until it caramelises.

Add the mushrooms to the onions. Add a pinch of salt and pepper and continue cooking till softened and coloured.

Once all the ingredients are cooked and cooled, place in a serving bowl with the silverbeet, coriander stems and basil. Toss well, then add the dressing and mix until it's well combined. Check the seasoning.

Top with the peanuts and Chang's fried noodles, and serve immediately. Add extra sliced chilli for colour and a little more heat.

NOTES If you are taking this to gathering, don't add the dressing or the fried noodles until you're about to serve it. ● You'll find black rice in mainstream supermarkets, as well as health food stores and Asian grocers. I use Forbidden Black Rice. ● Replace soy with tamari for a gluten-free option.

FEEDWELL TORTILLA

I live in Barcelona where tortilla is such a popular dish, though it's very rare that you would find a vegan tortilla in Spain. This recipe uses versatile chickpea flour – harina de garbanzos in Spanish. It's quick, easy and delicious. It's great for lunch served with a green salad, or cut into thin slices as part of a vegan tapas selection. **PICTURED ON PAGE 144**

SERVES 4

- 4 potatoes, peeled and cut into smallish chunks
- 1 cup chickpea flour
- salt and pepper
- 60 g baby spinach
- olive or vegetable oil, for frying
- green salad and tomato chutney, to serve

Place potatoes in a saucepan, cover with water and add 1 teaspoon of salt. Boil until just soft. It's important not to overcook them.

Whisk together chickpea flour, 1½ cups water and salt and pepper, making sure there are no lumps.

Drain potatoes and add more salt. The tortilla needs to be salty!

Add the chickpea batter and spinach, and gently mix together. Season to taste.

Heat a medium-sized frying pan and coat the bottom and sides with olive or vegetable oil. Add the batter and make sure it is evenly spread in the pan. Cook for about 12 minutes on medium heat.

You will notice the tortilla firming up. If you feel confident, gently slide a spatula all the way around the tortilla, turn it on to a plate and then flip the uncooked side, bottom down in the pan and cook for a further 5 minutes. Or you can place it under a hot grill for 5 minutes until the top is lightly browned.

The tortilla can be eaten hot, cold or at room temperature. Serve with a green salad. Tomato chutney works well too.

NOTES This is best eaten on the day, but can be kept in an airtight container in the fridge for a day. It can also be frozen for a month. ● If the tortilla is part of a tapas selection, top it with a vegan pesto.

PREVIOUS PAGE (clockwise from top left):

Feedwell Tortilla
Smoky Adzuki Bean Tempeh with Roasted Cauliflower, 143
Crunchy Black Rice Salad, 146

WEEKEND PIE

This is a great, easy recipe that I adapted from a friend's much-loved sausage roll recipe. Make it your own – you'll find your own favourite combination of vegetables. My family always requests this – as my grandson says, 'Anything with pastry has to be good.'

SERVES 8

- 1 carrot, diced
- 1 medium potato, peeled and diced
- 1 cup broccoli or cauliflower, chopped
- 1 tablespoon oil
- 1 onion, finely chopped
- 1 teaspoon curry powder
- ½ cup frozen peas or corn
- 1 x 400 g can lentils, drained
- ½ cup relish or chutney
- 2 sheets vegan puff pastry, thawed
- melted margarine or vegan butter, for brushing
- relish, chutney or tomato sauce, for serving

Preheat the oven to 200°C.

Steam the carrot, potato and broccoli or cauliflower till tender.

Heat the oil in a pan on medium heat and sauté the onion with the curry powder until the onion is soft.

In a large bowl, fold together the steamed vegies, peas or corn, cooked onion, drained lentils and relish or chutney. Do not over-stir.

Put one sheet of the pastry on baking paper on the bench and place half the vegie mixture down the centre. Fold the pastry over the mixture into an oblong, using a little water to help stick the pastry edge down to form a parcel. Repeat with remaining pastry and filling.

Use the baking paper to transfer the pies to a lined oven tray, making sure the seam is underneath.

Prick the parcel tops with a fork and, if you want to, brush with a little melted margarine.

Bake for 20 minutes or until pastry is golden.

Serve in slices with extra relish or chutney.

NOTES Leftovers will keep in an airtight container in the fridge for 2 days. ● The assembled pies can be frozen before cooking. ● This is a great way to use up any leftover vegetables.

CAULIFLOWER *and* CASHEW PASTRIES

This recipe is amazingly versatile. It's perfect for lunch with a side salad, or cut into smaller pastry shapes for a snack, or to shine as elegant finger food at a party. The cauliflower mixture is also delicious on toasted sourdough for breakfast! **PICTURED ON PAGE 151**

MAKES AT LEAST 8

- ½ head cauliflower, cut into small florets
- ½ small red onion, diced
- ⅓ cup raw cashews, chopped
- 3 tablespoons currants
- 1 tablespoons olive oil (can be omitted if avoiding oil)
- 1 teaspoon ground cumin
- 1 teaspoon dried or fresh thyme
- 1 teaspoon chilli flakes, or to taste
- 2 sheets frozen vegan puff pastry (see note)
- chopped parsley and drizzle of balsamic vinegar, to serve

Pre-heat oven to 200°C.

Steam cauliflower florets or cook for 1 minute in the microwave – just enough to take the edge off the raw crunch.

Gently microwave onion, or fry in oil or steam in a splash of water over low heat.

Combine all ingredients except pastry.

Cut the defrosted pastry into quarters and place on baking paper on an oven tray. Divide the cauliflower mixture between the pastry quarters, leaving a 1 cm border around the square.

Bake for 10–12 minutes until the pastry is cooked and golden.

Garnish with parsley, drizzle with balsamic vinegar and serve hot.

NOTES The cauliflower mixture can be made ahead and kept in an airtight container in the fridge for 24 hours – great pre-planning for a party! ● Pampas puff pastry is 25 cm, which cuts perfectly into four quarters, or smaller if making finger food for a party.

FOLLOWING PAGE (clockwise from top right):

Mushroom and Thyme Pate, 154
Crispy Crackers, 156
Cauliflower and Cashew Pastries
Carrot Top Pesto, 153
Not-sausage rolls, 152
Crowd-pleasing Carrot Cake, 179

NOT-SAUSAGE ROLLS

Our family always requests these for special events. If you don't have the vegies listed, you can substitute others. They're great on their own – don't forget the tomato sauce! – or with chips and salad, or even some black bean dhal. PICTURED ON PAGE 150

MAKES 16

- 2 sheets frozen vegan puff pastry
- 1 tablespoon cooking oil of your choice (I use avocado)
- 1 medium brown onion, finely diced
- 2 cloves garlic, minced
- 4–5 medium mushrooms, finely diced
- ½ teaspoon salt
- ½ teaspoon pepper
- 1 teaspoon paprika
- 400 g plant-based mince (I use Naturali)
- 3 large carrots, coarsely grated
- 1 teaspoon dried mixed herbs
- 1 teaspoon dried basil
- 2 tablespoons light soy sauce
- 2 tablespoons tomato sauce
- 1 teaspoon Dijon mustard
- 3–4 tablespoons breadcrumbs (I like the herb and garlic ones for extra flavour)
- 1 tablespoon sesame seeds (plus extra for garnish)
- tomato sauce, for serving

Thaw pastry according to packet instructions. Preheat oven to 200°C.

Heat oil over medium heat in a large frying pan. Gently fry the onion with the crushed garlic until translucent. Add the mushrooms to the pan, season with salt, pepper and paprika and continue frying until the mushrooms have reduced and are darker in colour. Stir regularly.

Add the mince, breaking it down so the mixture has an even consistency. Add the grated carrot and continue to fry. Add mixed herbs, basil, soy sauce, tomato sauce and Dijon mustard and continue to fry, stirring constantly. Taste and season with more salt and pepper if required.

Add sesame seeds and breadcrumbs, adjusting quantity of the breadcrumbs if the mixture looks excessively sloppy or too dry – it should have enough substance to hold its shape in a long sausage on the pastry. Remove from the heat and allow to cool for a few minutes.

Cut the first pastry sheet in half. Spoon mixture along one side, leaving approximately 1 cm between the mix and the edge of the pastry. Gently squeeze the mixture to form a roll, ensuring the roll is even along the entire length of the pastry all the way to the ends.

Gently roll the pastry around the mixture until it is fully enclosed. Seal the pastry edge, using a little water if needed, then cut each roll into four even 'sausage' rolls. Repeat with remaining pastry.

Pour a layer of sesame seeds into onto a plate, then firmly press the top of each roll into the seeds. I've found this delivers a better result than trying to evenly sprinkle sesame seeds over the top of each one.

Place the rolls onto a baking tray lined with baking paper and bake in the middle of the oven for 25 minutes or until golden brown.

Serve straight out of the oven.

CARROT TOP PESTO

I love pesto and use it in so many ways (on pasta, in risotto, dolloped over roasted vegies, spread over bagels, in sandwiches). This beautiful pesto uses the leafy green tops of carrots – it makes a beautiful vibrant green pesto with a nice hint of fresh lemon, and is a family favourite.

PICTURED ON PAGE 150

MAKES ABOUT 1 CUP

- 3 cups carrot top greens, washed with stems removed
- ¾ cup pistachios, shelled
- ½ clove garlic, minced
- 2 tablespoons nutritional yeast flakes (optional)
- pinch of salt
- zest and juice of 1 small lemon
- ½–¾ cup extra virgin olive oil

Add carrot top greens and the pistachios to a food processor and blend. If you like your pesto a little bit chunkier, save a couple of tablespoons of the pistachios and add them to the food processor at the very end.

Add the garlic, nutritional yeast flakes (if using), salt and the lemon zest and juice and blend further. Gradually add the olive oil, blending until you've got the right consistency, adding more oil if necessary.

Scoop pesto into a clean jar with a lid. Level the top of the pesto and then cover with a very thin layer of olive oil to seal out the air. Level the top and add more olive oil after every time you use it.

NOTES Pesto keeps in a sealed jar in the fridge for 7 to 10 days. It also freezes very well in a jar. ● If you don't have enough carrot top greens to make three cups, add basil or parsley leaves to make up the difference. ● The nutritional yeast adds a savoury cheese-like flavour, but this recipe is also good without it.

DAMIEN MANDER | FOUNDER, IAPF | @DAMIEN_MANDER

MUSHROOM *and* THYME PATE

I love to cook, but it's always off the cuff! Mushroom pate is one of my favourites –the essential flavourings for me are the brandy and thyme, but make this recipe your own. Use my notes as a starting point, have a go, and trust your judgement.

MAKES ABOUT 1 CUP

- 50 g walnuts
- 50 ml olive oil
- 50 ml brandy
- 120 g mushrooms, chopped
- ¼ brown onion, finely chopped
- minced garlic, to taste
- fresh thyme leaves, to taste
- salt and pepper
- thinly sliced toasted bread or crackers, to serve

Dry-roast the walnuts in a hot pan and then put to one side. Don't overdo it – you want them to be lightly toasted.

Heat the oil in a pan on medium heat, and gently cook the mushrooms, garlic and brandy.

Once the mushrooms are cooked, add the thyme to taste and cool to room temperature.

Blend the walnuts and the mushrooms to your preferred consistency – chunky or super smooth – adding a little more oil if required.

Season with salt and pepper, tasting to see if you need to add more thyme.

This is delicious with some crispy toasted bread or the crackers on page 156.

NOTES Swap the thyme for tarragon, sage or parsley, or use a mix of fresh herbs. • Swap the walnuts for cashews. • Add some truffle oil to taste.

CRISPY CRACKERS

These simple and tasty seedy crackers are a wonderful addition to any platter of nibblies. They also make a lovely homemade gift with a jar of pesto. **PICTURED ON PAGE 155**

MAKES A LOT

- ½ cup chia seeds (any colour)
- 1 large clove garlic, crushed
- 1 tablespoon fresh or dried woody herbs, such as rosemary
- pinch of sea salt
- ½ cup sunflower seeds
- ½ cup any combination of small seeds, such as sesame, flaxseed or poppy seeds
- ½ cup almond meal or LSA
- 2 tablespoons hemp seeds or nutritional yeast flakes (optional, for a more nutty or cheesy flavour)

Preheat the oven to 160°C. Line a tray with baking paper.

In a medium bowl, combine the chia, garlic, herbs, salt and 1 cup cold water. Whisk until the chia starts to soften and go gloopy.

Add the remaining ingredients and mix in well.

Spread out thinly and evenly on the lined tray, no more than 5 mm thick.

Bake for 25 minutes. Flip it, mark out a grid with a knife to help cut into crackers later, and bake the other side for 25 minutes. If not fully dried and crispy by this time, turn the oven off and let it sit in there till cool.

Cut along the marks. Enjoy the crackers as a snack on their own or serve with your favourite dips. They're great with Carrot Top Pesto (see page 153) or Mushroom Pate (see page 154).

NOTE Crackers will keep in an airtight container for 2 weeks (if they last that long).

MAPLE GLAZED CARROTS

I love Jamie Oliver's cooking. This is based on a recipe from Jamie's *Christmas Cookbook* (2016) that uses butter and honey but when I became vegan I need an alternative so that I could continue to enjoy his great recipes. I recommend veganising your favourite recipes – think creatively and you never need to feel like you're missing out.

SERVES 4–6

- about a kilo of organic carrots with tops still on
- 50–60 g non-dairy butter (I use Nuttelex)
- 6 cloves garlic, crushed but not peeled
- 8 sprigs thyme
- 2 good-sized oranges, juiced
- 2 fresh bay leaves or 4 dried
- about 3 tablespoons maple syrup
- salt and pepper

Trim and wash carrots, leaving a bit of the green on the top. Set aside some of the feathery ends for a garnish at the end.

Melt the butter in a large frying pan over medium heat, throw the garlic into the pan and turn after a minute. Sprinkle in the thyme sprigs (they will crackle – it sounds great!)

Pour in the orange juice, bay leaves, a splash of water and most of the maple syrup. Adjust the maple syrup to taste as you go.

Add the carrots with a generous pinch of salt and black pepper and jiggle the pan to coat the carrots.

Cover and reduce heat to medium–low for 10–15 minutes. Check taste, adding a little more maple syrup if you need to.

Uncover the pan and allow the liquid to reduce, ensuring that it doesn't evaporate completely. Add another splash of water if necessary. Once the carrots have a glazed look, the caramelisation is done and you can serve.

Pile the carrots on a serving plate, with some feathery carrot tops for garnish.

NOTES The carrots will keep in an airtight container in the fridge for a couple of days. ● Use some purple or yellow heirloom carrots as well if you can find them – they make a wonderful display. ● You can use about 8 tablespoons of bottled orange juice, but fresh juice is better. ● Use the tops to make the delicious Carrot Top Pesto on page 153.

CRISPY SALT *and* PEPPER TOFU

Years ago, every Tuesday I would grab the free music mag, go to Happy Chef in Newtown, order their Salt and Pepper Tofu, read the mag and figure out which gigs to go to. My weekly routine was such that the man who took my order would say to me, 'Same, same.' After I moved away, I was forced to create my own version. (Unfortunately, poor old Happy Chef has since burned down.)

SERVES 2–4

- 500 g silken tofu
- ½ cup cornflour
- 1 teaspoon ground white pepper
- 1 teaspoon salt
- 1 teaspoon garlic salt
- rice bran oil, for frying

Garnish

- 1 teaspoon sesame oil
- 1 teaspoon rice bran oil
- 2 long red chillies, sliced
- 1 bird's eye chilli, sliced (optional, if you like an extra chilli hit)
- 3 large cloves garlic, chopped
- 2 spring onions, sliced

To serve

- Szechuan pepper
- steamed rice
- soy sauce

To get the best result, first press the excess water out of the tofu. Remove tofu from packet and drain, then put onto a plate. Cover with another plate, then place a weight on top and leave to sit for 20 minutes. You can use anything as a weight – I use a heavy bowl.

While the tofu is being pressed, prepare the garnish. In a small frying pan, heat the sesame seed oil and rice bran oil. Add the chopped chillies, garlic and spring onions. Stir for about 5 minutes on medium heat until onions have softened and garlic has turned golden. Set aside.

To prepare tofu coating, combine cornflour, white pepper, salt and garlic salt in a medium ziplock bag and give it a good shake to mix.

Remove weight and plate from tofu and drain. Cut drained tofu into bite-size triangles.

In a large frying pan on medium–high heat, add rice bran oil to a depth of 1½–2 cm and heat.

Drop tofu pieces gently into the ziplock bag a few at a time, coating all sides. Drop into the hot oil. Repeat with remaining tofu. Fry until crispy and pale golden colour on all sides.

To finish, sprinkle with the prepared garnish and a generous pinch of Szechuan pepper. Serve straight away with steamed rice, and soy sauce on the side.

'Being vegan means
I walk my talk in
all aspects of this:
first, do no harm.'

SHARLOT CLARK

Recipe list

SOMETHING *Sweet*

Treat time –
cakes, biscuits *and*
desserts *to* share

CHOC-CARAMEL KINGSTON CRUNCH

As a qualified nutritionist and food scientist, I believe that reducing total sugars and glycemic load is beneficial for long-term health. However, I also have a bit of a chocolate and caramel obsession. The crunch from the maple cashews in this recipe is unreal – this slice reminds me of Arnott's Kingston biscuits (without the glycemic load).

MAKES 16–24 SQUARES

Base layer

- ½ cup maple-roasted cashews
- ½ cup dry-roasted cashews
- ½ cup All-Bran (or gluten-free rice bran sticks)
- ½ cup shredded coconut
- 2 heaped tablespoons pure cocoa or cacao
- 2 heaped tablespoons powdered low-calorie natural sweetener
- ½ cup coconut oil, melted

Caramel layer

- 125 g coconut oil
- ⅔ cup sugar-free maple syrup
- ⅓ cup natural crunchy peanut butter
- 1 tablespoon powdered low-calorie natural sweetener
- pinch of salt

Top layer

- 200 g low-sugar dark chocolate
- 60 g coconut oil
- fresh berries, to serve

FOR THE BASE LAYER, line an 18 × 18 cm square slice tin with baking paper.

In a high-speed blender, blitz the maple-roasted cashews, dry-roasted cashews and All-Bran into crumbs. Place crumbs in mixing bowl and combine with cocoa, powdered sweetener and shredded coconut.

Melt the coconut oil in a microwave or on the stovetop and mix with the crumbs. Press base mixture evenly into the slice tin. Refrigerate to set while preparing next layer.

FOR THE CARAMEL LAYER, combine the coconut oil, maple syrup, peanut butter and sweetener (omit sweetener if using regular maple syrup) and melt gently in a microwave or on the stovetop.

Pour caramel sauce over base. Allow to set in refrigerator.

FOR THE CHOCOLATE LAYER, break chocolate blocks into pieces, and place in a microwave-safe glass jug along with the coconut oil. Melt in intermittent bursts. Alternatively, this can be done in a heatproof bowl over a simmering pot of water on the stovetop.

When the caramel layer has set, pour the melted chocolate on top of the slice and evenly distribute by tilting the tin gently from side to side. Place in refrigerator and allow to set for at least 2 hours.

With a hot sharp knife, cut into 16 portions or 24 pieces, depending on your size preference. Serve straight from the fridge with coffee or tea and some fresh berries.

CHOCOLATE FUDGE BROWNIE

Being in the health and fitness industry, I'm very aware that there is almost just as much junk food out there for us vegans now as there is non-vegans, so I try to focus on food as fuel as well as enjoyment. Not only is this brownie delicious, it's packed full of protein and healthy fats – and is also free of refined sugar and gluten. Something to appeal to your sweet tooth while being good for you!

MAKES 16 SQUARES

- 1 cup cooked and mashed pumpkin
- 2 scoops chocolate protein powder
- ½ cup almond butter
- ¼ cup raw cacao
- 2 tablespoons rice malt syrup
- ½ cup sugar-free dark chocolate, chopped

Preheat the oven to 180°C. Line a brownie pan with baking paper.

Place the pumpkin, protein powder, almond butter, cacao and syrup in a large bowl and mix well until you have a smooth consistency.

Smooth the mixture into the pan, making sure it is evenly spread.

Bake for 12–15 minutes, then remove and allow to cool in the tin.

Meanwhile, place the chocolate in a heatproof bowl over simmering water, making sure the water doesn't touch the bottom of the bowl. Stir until melted. When the baked brownie is cool, spread the chocolate evenly over the top.

Refrigerate to set before cutting into squares.

NOTE Brownies will keep in an airtight container in the fridge for 3 days. They can also be frozen.

ARLO'S COCONUT *and* CACAO BICKIES

These bickies have been a staple of our cafe cabinet since day one because they're healthy, filling and, above all, delicious!

MAKES 20–24

- 2 cups brown sugar
- 1 cup coconut oil, melted
- 1 cup rice bran oil
- 1 cup coconut milk
- 1 cup shredded coconut
- 1 cup cacao nibs
- 1 cup rolled oats
- 1½ teaspoons baking powder
- 3 cups flour
- 1 teaspoon sea salt

Preheat oven to 190°C and line one or two trays with baking paper.

Place the sugar, oils and coconut milk into a big mixing bowl and stir.

Add all the other ingredients and get your clean hands in there for a good smoosh-up! If you think the mixture is a bit sloppy, add a little more flour.

Once you have a well-combined dough, divide into about 24 balls. Place 3 cm apart on a baking tray and press down to make a biscuit shape (flat and roundish).

Bake for 18–20 minutes or until golden. Cool for 5 minutes on the tray. Repeat with remaining dough.

Enjoy with a mug of your favourite tea!

NOTE Bickies will keep in an airtight container for 5 days.

AMANDA LOGAN | @MYGOODNESSKITCHEN

STICKY DATE CAKE *with* SALTED CARAMEL FROSTING

This easy cake balances sweet dates with a wicked salted caramel frosting – it's like a big vegan kiss in the taste buds. Let the love begin!

SERVES 10–12

Cake

- 250 g dates, weighed before pitting (12–13 dates)
- 1 teaspoon bicarbonate of soda
- 1¼ cup plain flour
- 2 teaspoons baking powder
- pinch of fine sea salt
- 1 teaspoon vanilla extract
- ⅓ cup raw sugar
- ⅓ cup olive oil
- ¾ cup soy or almond milk
- ⅓ cup flaked almonds (optional)

FOR THE CAKE, pre-heat oven to 180°C. Line a 22-cm round cake tin with baking paper.

Remove the pits from the dates and pop them in a heatproof bowl with 1 cup boiling water and the bicarbonate of soda and stand for 5 minutes.

Combine the flour, baking powder and salt in a large mixing bowl

Pulse the dates a few times (6 or 7 quick pulses) with a stick blender. Add the vanilla, sugar, oil and milk and stir to combine. (The oil won't completely combine – it doesn't matter).

Stir the wet ingredients in to the flour until just combined.

Pour the cake batter in to the prepared tin and bake for 45–50 minutes or until a cake tester comes out clean. At around the 30-minute mark when the top of the cake is set, gently cover the cake with foil to slow the browning process.

Remove the cake from the oven and let it stand for 10 minutes before removing it from the tin. Allow it to cool completely.

CONTINUED >

Salted caramel sauce

- 400 ml full-fat coconut milk
- ¾ cup rapadura or coconut sugar
- 2 tablespoons vegan butter spread
- 1 teaspoon vanilla extract
- 1 teaspoon fine sea salt

Frosting

- 3 cups icing sugar, sifted
- 4 tablespoons vegan butter spread
- 2 tablespoons plant-based milk
- ¼ cup salted caramel sauce

FOR THE SALTED CARAMEL SAUCE, place the coconut milk and sugar in a heavy-bottomed saucepan. Bring to the boil over medium heat, stirring. Reduce the heat and simmer for 30 minutes, stirring frequently.

When the sauce has thickened and is a lovely amber colour, stir in the butter, vanilla and sea salt. Remove from the heat and cool.

FOR THE FROSTING, combine the icing sugar, softened butter and milk in the large bowl of a stand mixer and whip to combine. When the frosting is thick and fluffy, add ¼ cup of the cooled sauce and whip again to combine.

Add more icing sugar if needed to make a thick frosting.

To finish, slather the cooled cake with the salted caramel frosting and a sprinkling of flaked almonds. For added flair, swirl the remaining caramel sauce over the cake when serving.

NOTES The cake is best eaten on the day but will keep in an airtight container in the fridge for up to 3 days. • This cake is also wonderful with a simple dusting of icing sugar.

MORGAN'S PRE-RACE DATES

This recipe is based on one from Gojé Frozen Yoghurt in Yarraville in Melbourne where everything is plant-based and made from scratch. I love these chocolate-coated dates because they're delicious and quick and easy to make. I eat them for energy before I train or race and I also like to have them as a dessert.

MAKES 6

- 6 medjool dates, pitted
- 1 x block organic vegan dark chocolate
- peanut butter (I use Mayver's)

Cut an opening in each date with a knife and stuff with peanut butter (as much as you desire). Press the date closed.

Heat a few centimetres of water in a small saucepan until it's simmering.

Chop the chocolate and place it in a heatproof bowl that will fit over the saucepan without touching the water.

Stir the chocolate gently to melt. Once melted, remove from heat.

Roll the dates in the dark chocolate and place on baking paper, then refrigerate until firm.

Once set, take out of fridge and enjoy. If you have leftover chocolate, make more dates!

NOTE The dates will keep in an airtight container in the fridge for a week.

DANI RAULLI

SPICED PINEAPPLE TEACAKE

Cakes have always been my favourite thing to make, and that hasn't changed since going vegan two years ago. This is a twist on a Jewish honey cake, but kind to bees! It's super quick to put together, perfect if you need a dessert in a hurry, or an afternoon treat or a sweet brekkie. Serve it with fresh berries or even a vegan passionfruit curd. It's quite sweet, so anything tart works well with it. **PICTURED ON PAGE 175**

SERVES 8

- 1 tablespoon flaxseed meal
- 220 g plain flour
- ½ teaspoon baking powder
- ½ teaspoon bicarbonate of soda
- ¼ teaspoon salt
- 1½ teaspoons ground cinnamon
- ¼ teaspoon ground cloves
- ¼ teaspoon ground allspice
- 140 g white sugar
- 45 g brown sugar
- 115 ml sunflower oil (or any light vegetable oil)
- ½ cup rice malt syrup
- 100 ml strong fruity tea, warm but not hot
- 100 ml pineapple juice
- ½ teaspoon vanilla extract

To serve

dried pineapple slices, fresh berries, vegan passionfruit curd or a scoop of vegan vanilla ice-cream

Preheat oven to 180°C. Grease a standard loaf tin with a little vegan butter (or cooking spray if you're lazy like me!) Line with baking paper. This is a sticky cake, so don't skip this part.

Make a flax egg by mixing the flaxseed meal with 3 tablespoons water. Leave to thicken while you make the cake.

In a large bowl, whisk together the flour, baking powder, bicarbonate of soda, salt, spices and sugars.

In another bowl whisk together oil, rice malt syrup, tea, pineapple juice and vanilla.

Mix together the wet and dry ingredients. Mix in the flax egg until all the ingredients are well combined.

Bake for 40 to 50 minutes. The cake is cooked if it springs back when pressed lightly, or if a cake tester comes out clean. Let it cool slightly before turning out onto a rack to cool completely.

Serve with dried pineapple slices, fresh berries, vegan passionfruit curd or a scoop of vegan vanilla ice-cream.

NOTES This cake keeps in an airtight container for a few days. • Make two smaller loaves – one to keep and one to give away. • I use Red Seal Peach & Pineapple tea.

CHOC BERRY CRUMBLE SLICE

I have the lovely Bhavani Baumann from the Green Lion to thank for this recipe – a slice that doubles as a dessert! When they had to close their venue, Bhavani and her family forged ahead, delivering their scrumptious food to happy Sydneysiders. Green Lion meals are available at the Cruelty Free Shop. PICTURED ON PAGE 174

SERVES 6

Base & topping

- 1 cup caster sugar
- 1 teaspoon baking powder
- 3 cups plain flour
- ¼ teaspoon salt
- finely grated zest of 1 small lemon (optional)
- 250 g cold vegan butter (I use Nuttelex)
- 1 serve vegan egg replacer
- ½ teaspoon pure vanilla extract

Berry filling

- 4½ cups chopped fresh berries (one type or a mixture)
- ½ cup sugar
- 4 teaspoons cornflour
- juice of 1 small lemon
- ½ cup grated dark chocolate
- non-dairy vanilla ice cream, to serve

Preheat oven to 180°C. For a slice, line a 20 × 30 cm pan with baking paper. For a dessert, use a round overproof dish.

FOR THE BASE AND TOPPING, use a hand mixer or stand mixer fitted with the paddle attachment. Combine the sugar, baking powder, flour and salt, add the lemon zest (if using), butter, egg replacement and vanilla and beat on low speed until the butter is evenly distributed and the mixture is crumbly. If you don't have a mixer, you can get a good result by rubbing the mixture between your fingers.

Put a little more than half of the mixture into the bottom of the prepared pan. Use your hand or the bottom of a measuring cup to evenly press the dough into the pan.

FOR THE FILLING, gently stir together all ingredients until everything is evenly distributed.

Spread the filling over the crust, then spread the chocolate flakes evenly. Crumble the remaining dough over the top of the berries.

Bake for approximately 40 minutes, until the top is light golden brown.

Transfer the pan to rack to cool.

Serve warm with vanilla ice cream and a sprinkle of cocoa powder or icing sugar, or cut into squares when cooled for afternoon tea.

NOTES The slice will keep in an airtight container in the fridge for a couple of days. • Frozen berries can be used, but it will be a wetter crumble. • The lemon is optional in the base mixture but adds a lovely flavour.

ULTIMATE CHOCOLATE CHUNK COOKIES

This is my favourite cookie recipe, producing large, chewy cookies with crispy edges. Everyone I've made them for has loved them. The recipe has been adapted from a *New York Times* recipe by David Leite to be vegan, among other tweaks. PICTURED ON PAGE 175

MAKES 20 LARGE OR 30 REGULAR

- 240 g plain flour
- 240 g bread flour (00 flour)
- 1¼ teaspoons bicarbonate of soda
- 1½ teaspoons baking powder
- 1½ teaspoons salt
- 290 g vegan butter (I use Nuttelex Buttery)
- 290 g brown sugar
- 230 g granulated sugar
- 2 teaspoons egg replacer (I use Orgran No Egg)
- 2 teaspoons vanilla essence
- 400 g vegan dark chocolate, cut into chunks
- coarse sea salt (optional)

Preheat oven to 200°C and line two trays with baking paper.

In a large bowl, sift both flours, bicarbonate of soda, baking powder and salt.

Put butter and both sugars In the bowl of a stand mixer and cream with the paddle attachment for 5 minutes.

Mix the egg replacer with 4 tablespoons water to make a paste. Add to the butter and sugar with the vanilla and mix for a further minute, scraping down sides.

Add dry ingredients and mix until just combined. Fold in chocolate chunks with a spatula.

Using an ice-cream scoop, scoop generous balls of dough and place on trays, leaving plenty of space for spreading. Sprinkle coarse sea salt on top and bake for 18–20 mins or until the edges are golden. The cookies will harden when cooling down.

Allow cookies to cool for 5 minutes on trays before transferring to a wire rack. Repeat with remaining dough.

NOTES The cookies will keep in an airtight container for at least one week. The dough can be frozen. ● Use a tablespoon to scoop smaller cookies. Bake for 12–15 minutes. ● Any vegan dark chocolate will work. My favourites are Aldi Dairy Fine dark chocolate and Coles Belgium Dark Chocolate. ● Use 200 g vegan white chocolate and 200 g roughly chopped macadamias instead of the dark chocolate. This will produce a chewier cookie that is equally delicious.

SPICED CARAMEL PEAR TARTS

This amazing decadent dessert is a go-to recipe whenever I need to whip up an impressive dessert. It looks much harder than it is to make! The pears are poached with all my favourite warming spices, and the filling is ever so creamy. PICTURED ON PAGE 175

SERVES 6–8

Crust

- 1½ cups rolled oats
- 2 tablespoons coconut sugar (or brown sugar)
- 60 g coconut oil
- 1 tablespoon lemon juice
- a pinch of salt

Filling

- 1½ cups full-fat coconut milk
- 3 tablespoons brown sugar
- 3 tablespoons lemon juice
- 2 teaspoons agar agar
- 1 teaspoon tapioca starch
- ½ teaspoon salt
- ½ cup shredded coconut

FOR THE CRUST, preheat oven to 180°C.

Blend the rolled oats in a food processor till it becomes a rough flour. Add the sugar, coconut oil, lemon juice and salt. Blend, slowly adding 4–6 tablespoons water one at a time until a dough forms.

Press the dough into greased individual tart tins, or use small pie dishes or muffin trays.

Bake for 20–25 minutes until the crust is golden and crunchy.

Cool for about 1 hour before filling.

FOR THE FILLING, mix the coconut milk, sugar, lemon juice, agar agar, tapioca starch and salt in a saucepan over low heat until everything is completely dissolved.

Turn up the heat and bring to the boil, stirring constantly for a minute or two. Reduce heat and simmer for 2–3 minutes while still stirring.

Add the shredded coconut and stir.

Pour the filling into the crusts and refrigerate for an hour.

CONTINUED >

PREVIOUS PAGE (clockwise from top right):
Ultimate Chocolate Chunk Cookies , 176
Spiced Caramel Pear Tarts
Spiced Pineapple Teacake, 172
Choc Berry Crumble Slice, 173

Caramel sauce

6–8 medjool dates

Poached pears

3 pears, de-cored and cut into eighths

3–4 cinnamon sticks

3 tablespoons brown sugar

1 teaspoon vanilla essence

1 teaspoon cloves

1 teaspoon nutmeg

1 teaspoon allspice

6 star anise

coconut yoghurt or dairy-free ice-cream, to serve

FOR THE CARAMEL SAUCE, blend dates and 4 tablespoons water until they form a creamy liquid. Add more water if needed. Set aside.

FOR THE POACHED PEARS, combine the pears, sugar, all the spices and about ½ cup of water in a saucepan over medium heat. Bring to the boil and cook the pears for about 5 minutes, then reduce the heat and cover with a lid.

Let the pears simmer and poach until they are soft and the water is absorbed. Check them after 15 minutes – you want them to hold their shape. Add water as needed. Drain the pears and cool to room temperature.

Top the tarts with pears just before serving.

Drizzle caramel sauce over the tarts, and serve with coconut yoghurt or dairy-free ice-cream.

NOTES The tarts will keep in an airtight container in the fridge for 5 days. • You can make one tart using a greased springform tin.

CROWD-PLEASING CARROT CAKE

I've always loved carrot cake so one of the first things I did when I became vegan is develop my own version without dairy. Over time I've added the delicious peanut butter frosting – now it's essential!

PICTURED ON PAGE 150

SERVES 10

- 125 ml coconut oil, melted
- 125 ml rice bran oil
- 300 g brown sugar
- 1½ teaspoons vanilla essence
- 200 ml almond milk
- 450 g plain flour
- 1½ teaspoons baking powder
- 1½ teaspoons bicarbonate of soda
- 1 teaspoon cinnamon
- 2 teaspoons ground ginger
- ½ teaspoon nutmeg
- 30 g shredded coconut
- 1 orange, zest only, finely grated
- 270 g carrot, peeled and grated
- 75 g pecans, chopped
- 50 g glace ginger, finely chopped

Icing

- 150 g vegan butter (I use Nuttelex Buttery)
- 50 g smooth peanut butter
- 2–3 tablespoons almond milk
- 300 g icing sugar, sifted

Decoration

edible flowers, shredded coconut, chopped nuts, chopped glace ginger, candied citrus zest

FOR THE CAKE, preheat the oven to 180°C. Grease and line bottom and sides of 2 × 20-centimetre cake tins.

Whisk the oils and sugar together, then add the vanilla and milk in a large bowl.

Combine the flour, baking powder, bicarbonate of soda, spices, coconut and orange zest in a separate bowl. Add to the wet ingredients and mix till well combined. Stir in the carrot, nuts and ginger. Add a little more flour if the mixture is a bit loose.

Divide the mixture between the two tins and bake for 35–40 minutes until a skewer inserted into the middle of the cakes comes out clean. Cool the cakes in the tins for about 10 minutes, then carefully transfer to a wire rack to cool completely.

FOR THE ICING, combine the butter and peanut butter, beating with a fork until reasonably smooth. Whisk into the icing sugar, gradually adding the milk until it's the desired consistency. Make the icing quite thick for joining the cakes – you can add a little more milk later for the top layer. Leave in the fridge until needed.

TO ASSEMBLE, put one cake on a serving platter, flat side up, and spread with half the icing. Carefully place the second cake on top. Loosen the remaining icing with a little with extra milk if it's too thick, and cover the top. Decorate with your preferred toppings.

NOTES The cake will keep in an airtight container in the fridge for up to 3 days. ● You can also make this as a single layer slab cake – I make it in a 20 × 30 cm tin and cook it for a bit longer. Cut into squares.

CHOCOLATE *and* SOUR CREAM CAKE

This is a beautiful, rich and decadent cake – it's been one of the most popular recipes on my Sweet Lancey blog. The leftover chocolate glaze can also be drizzled on your favourite vegan desserts.

SERVES 10

- 260 g plain flour
- 210 g caster sugar (or more, if you like your cakes sweet)
- 60 g cocoa powder
- 1 tablespoon Greek ground coffee
- 1 teaspoon baking powder
- ½ teaspoon bicarbonate of soda
- 320 ml almond milk
- ¼ cup vegan sour cream (I used Dibble)
- sliced strawberries, to serve

Glaze

- 2 tablespoons liquid glucose, warm
- 1 tablespoons vegan milk
- 1½ tablespoons cocoa powder
- ½ tablespoon brown sugar

Preheat oven to 190°C and grease a bundt tin.

In a large bowl, sift together the flour, sugar, cocoa powder, coffee, baking powder and bicarbonate of soda until there are no lumps.

Slowly add the milk and sour cream, and mix until just combined. If your mixture is too thick (it should be thick but still easy to mix) add a little more milk.

Pour into prepared tin and bake for approximately 45 minutes, or until an inserted cake tester comes out clean.

Remove from the oven, and cool for 30 minutes before carefully removing from the cake tin.

FOR THE GLAZE, combine all ingredients in a bowl and mix until smooth.

Drizzle over the cake, top with strawberries and serve

NOTE The cake keeps well in an airtight container in the fridge for 5 days, or for 1 month in the freezer. Bring to room temperature for serving.

'Being vegan *simplifies* my life.'

SIDDHISVARI BULLOCH

Recipe list

CHOCOLATE SALTY BALLS

ANZAC SANDWICHES

NAN'S BANANA CAKE

MAPLE BAKED GRANOLA

SOUL-REVIVING RATATOUILLE

THE BEST LENTIL SOUP EVER

HUNGARIAN-STYLE SOUPY STEW

KINDNESS CASSOULET

NOURISHING MILLET CHILLI

RASCALLY DOG BISCUITS

GIFTS *of* Kindness

Nourish your soul *with* rice, soups and salads

CHOCOLATE SALTY BALLS

My inspiration came from the *South Park* 'Chocolate Salty Balls' song and my husband's love of chocolate/peanut butter, sweet/savoury and bitter/sweet flavour combinations. I love making these for friends when they're feeling down, because chocolate fixes almost anything. **PICTURED ON PAGE 190**

MAKES 20

- ¾ cup peanut butter (see notes)
- 1 cup Rice Bubbles
- 2 tablespoons icing sugar
- 150 g dairy-free dark chocolate, at least 70% cocoa
- sea salt flakes, for garnish

Place the peanut butter, Rice Bubbles and icing sugar into a large bowl. Mix till well combined. (I find that using a scraper for this is really handy, as it helps you get the peanut butter off the sides of the bowl.)

Place the bowl in the freezer for 15–20 minutes to chill.

Once the mixture is chilled, form into balls by rolling tablespoon-size portions of it between your palms. If it gets too sticky, simply rinse your hands in water. Leave your hands a little wet and continue balling.

Place the balls back in the freezer for another 20 minutes until firm – this way they're easier to coat in the chocolate.

Line a tray with baking paper.

Melt the chocolate in a heatproof bowl over simmering water, or in the microwave. Pop a ball into the chocolate and, using a fork, roll it around until it's coated. Remove any excess chocolate by scraping the underside of the fork on the edge of the bowl.

Place on the tray and sprinkle a little salt on the top. Repeat till all the balls are coated. (Don't stress if your chocolate-coating isn't perfect – your technique will improve each time you do it.)

Put the balls in the fridge to allow the chocolate to set before serving.

NOTES The recipe is easy to double, which means these are also great as a sweet offering at any gathering. Just keep them chilled in warmer weather as the chocolate will melt. ● Natural peanut butter is too earthy a flavour and too heavy in texture here. Use the more processed brands for this recipe.

ANZAC SANDWICHES

When I was living in London, Grandma used to send Anzacs in the mail, carefully wrapped. To me, they're such a taste of Australia! This was easy to veganise, and when I really want to impress, I sandwich them together with Biscoff, a surprise vegan treat! PICTURED ON PAGE 190

MAKES 10–12 SANDWICHES

- 1 cup rolled oats
- ¾ cup coconut, dessicated or shredded
- 1 cup raw sugar
- 1 cup plain flour, sifted
- 125 g vegan butter (I use Nuttelex Buttery)
- 2 tablespoons golden syrup
- ½ teaspoon bicarbonate of soda
- Lotus Biscoff spread, for filling

Preheat the oven to 180°C. Lined two baking trays with baking paper.

Place the oats, coconut, sugar and flour in a bowl and stir to combine.

Melt the butter and golden syrup in a saucepan over low heat.

In a separate bowl, combine the bicarbonate of soda and 3 tablespoons boiling water, then add to the buttery mixture. The mixture will froth up. Pour quickly into the dry ingredients and stir until well combined.

Roll heaped tablespoons of the mixture into 20–24 balls and place on the baking trays, allowing room for spreading.

Bake for 15 to 18 minutes, or until golden brown.

When the biscuits are cool, sandwich pairs together with a tablespoon of Biscoffe.

NOTES The biscuits will keep in an airtight container for a week or more ● Biscoff is available in most supermarkets. ● Make bigger Anzacs if you're not making sandwiches. ● Vary the cooking time according to whether you like your Anzacs chewy or crunchy. They're better a little bit crunchy for sandwiches.

NAN'S BANANA CAKE

I adapted this simple and delicious banana cake from my great-grandmother's recipe. We make it every day at Wombat Cafe. This is one of those recipes where the least effort seems to produce the best results – it takes less than five minutes to prepare, perfect for when unexpected visitors call in! My nan was a remarkable woman and an amazing cook, and I think of her every time I bake this cake. **PICTURED ON PAGE 191**

SERVES 6–8

- 1–2 ripe bananas, mashed (the riper the better)
- 1 teaspoon vanilla essence
- 1 cup sugar
- 1 cup self-raising flour (can substitute gluten-free flour)
- ½ cup soy milk
- 60 g vegan butter, melted (I use Nuttelex)

Icing

- 1 cup icing sugar, sifted
- juice of 1 lemon
- 1–2 tablespoons vegan butter
- 1–2 tablespoons soy milk
- walnuts and shredded coconut, to decorate

Preheat oven to 180°C. Lined a loaf tin with baking paper.

Mash the banana and add the vanilla.

Add the sugar, flour, milk and melted butter.

Mix until just combined.

Bake for around 30 minutes or until a cake tester comes out clean. Allow to cool completely before icing.

FOR THE ICING, combine icing sugar and lemon juice in a bowl and add the vegan butter until you get the desired consistency. Add a little milk to thin as required.

Spread over completely cooled cake and top with walnuts and a little shredded coconut. It's also delicious served warm with vegan butter, like a banana bread.

NOTES The cake keeps well in an airtight container for several days. It also freezes well. ● The cooking time will vary a little according to how many bananas you use and how ripe they are. ● Passionfruit pulp works well on top of the icing, or make passionfruit icing.

MAPLE BAKED GRANOLA

This will get you up and at 'em! If I have to do breakfast on the go then granola is my go-to. I just pack some into a container with my favourite fruit and some dairy-free yoghurt and I'm set for getting through a busy morning. Make a decent size batch of this as it keeps well. Switch ingredients such as nuts, seeds or dried fruit depending on what you fancy.

PICTURED ON PAGE 191

MAKES 1.2 KILOS

- 25 g puffed quinoa
- 40 g cocoa nibs
- 300 g rolled oats
- 100 g sunflower seeds
- 50 g pumpkin seeds
- 50 g sesame seeds
- 100 g almonds, skin on, coarsely chopped
- 50 g walnuts, coarsely chopped
- 1 teaspoon salt
- 1 teaspoon ground cinnamon
- 1 teaspoon ground ginger
- 75 g vegan butter (I use Nuttelex)
- 200 g maple syrup
- 50 g cranberries, dried
- 50 g golden raisins
- 50 g currants
- 10 g freeze-dried strawberry slices
- 50 g flaked coconut

Preheat the oven to 170°C.

Mix the quinoa, nibs, oats, sunflower, pumpkin and sesame seeds, almonds, walnuts, salt and spices together well in a large bowl.

Melt the butter in a large saucepan and add the maple syrup. Bring to a boil and remove from the heat. Leave to sit for five minutes before pouring onto the dry ingredients, mixing well with a wooden spoon, spatula or paddle attachment in a mixer.

Sprinkle the granola evenly onto baking trays lined with baking paper and bake for 18 minutes or until golden brown. Make sure the granola is cooked sufficiently to ensure you get crunchy clusters.

Leave to cool on the tray, then break the granola pieces into a container with the remaining ingredients and mix well.

Serve with seasonal fruits and dairy-free yoghurt for a fantastic start to the day.

NOTE Granola will keep in an airtight container in the pantry for up to 4 weeks.

FOLLOWING PAGE (clockwise from top right):

Maple Baked Granola
Soul-reviving Ratatouille, 192
Nan's Banana Cake, 188
Anzac Sandwiches, 187
Chocolate Salty Balls, 186

RACHAEL GERMANO | @THE_VEGANISTA_SISTA

SOUL-REVIVING RATATOUILLE

This is based on the ratatouille recipe from *Living the GI Diet* by Rick Gallop, with my own tweaks and notes. It's my go-to recipe for all occasions, whether I need a get-well casserole, a hearty nutrient boost on a Sunday afternoon, or a bit of extra help from 'Nature's broom'. I have been making this dish for 15 years, and it's a sure-fire hit with vegans and omnivores alike. **PICTURED ON PAGE 191**

SERVES 4–6

- generous dash of olive oil
- 1 large onion, chopped
- 4 cloves garlic, crushed
- half a fennel bulb, diced (if unavailable, substitute celery)
- 1 teaspoon herbes de Provence
- 1 x 400 g can diced tomatoes
- 1 teaspoon smoked paprika
- ¾ teaspoon fine Himalayan black salt
- 500 ml vegetable stock
- 1 large eggplant, diced
- 2 zucchini, diced
- 1 red capsicum, diced
- 2 x 400 g cans 4-bean mix, drained
- 350 g sweet chilli diced tofu nuggets (but any chunky diced tofu will do)
- 15 g flat-leaf parsley, roughly chopped
- salt and pepper

Heat the oil over medium-high heat in a large stockpot or wok.

Cook the onion, garlic, fennel and herbes de Provence for 5 mins, or until starting to brown. Add tomatoes, smoked paprika, black salt and stock, and bring to the boil.

Add the eggplant, zucchini, capsicum, beans and tofu; return to the boil. Reduce heat and simmer for about 30 minutes or until slightly thickened and the eggplant is tender.

Add parsley, season with salt and pepper, and serve.

NOTES The ratatouille keeps in an airtight container in the fridge for up to 5 days. ● Mix through ½ cup of brown rice if you have more mouths to feed. ● Herbes de Provence can be substituted for a mix of basil, thyme and oregano. But we try to keep it French, yes? ● Himalayan black salt can be found at your local delicatessen, or in the deli section of all good supermarkets. ● Substitute one can of 4-bean mix (or both!) with a can of red kidney beans, or chickpeas. Both are amazing and the texture blends perfectly.

LIZ VERCOE

THE BEST LENTIL SOUP EVER

I've been making lentil soup in various guises for over 30 years. This recipe is a game changer – it's my variation on the great man Yotam Ottolenghi's Curried Lentil, Tomato and Coconut Soup from *Simple*. I'm an impatient cook and often seek to adapt recipes to the least number of minutes and pots required! It's delicious. It's hearty. It's nutritious. It's *easy*. It's genuine comfort food. I make it in huge quantities and freeze it, give it away to those in need, and eat it for breakfast, lunch, dinner and in between.

SERVES 6

- 80 ml olive oil
- 2 onions, finely diced
- 3 tablespoons curry powder
- 1 teaspoon ground turmeric
- 1 tablespoon ground coriander (optional)
- 1 teaspoon chilli flakes
- 4 teaspoons garlic, chopped or crushed
- 6 teaspoons ginger, chopped or grated
- 2 cups red lentils, washed and drained
- 600 mls tomato passata
- handful of fresh coriander, leaves and stalks
- 2 x 400 ml tins coconut milk or cream
- salt and pepper

To serve

- basmati rice or pita bread
- coriander leaves

Heat the oil in a heavy-based saucepan and gently fry the onion for about 10 minutes.

Add the curry powder, turmeric, coriander if using, chilli flakes, garlic and ginger, and stir for a minute or two.

Add the lentils and passata and 1.5 litres water. Add coriander leaves and stalks (remember to save a couple of nice leaves for serving) and bring to the boil.

Turn down to the lowest heat, add coconut milk or cream, pop a lid on and cook for 30 minutes.

Serve the soup with coriander leaves for a nourishing lunch, or with basmati rice, homemade pita bread or anything your little heart desires.

NOTE If there's any left, it will keep in an airtight container in the fridge for several days and freezes well.

CAROLE MEADE | @VEGANDELICIOUSKYNETON

HUNGARIAN-STYLE SOUPY STEW

The team at Edgar's Mission would like to thank Carole, a very special lady who warms our hearts, souls and bellies on a weekly basis with her mouth-watering creations. Her generosity and kindness to us is a reminder of how much it means to be on the receiving end of the gift of food: it brightens our day. Thank you, Aunty Carole, from the bottom of our hearts.

SERVES 4 HUNGRY PEOPLE

- 2 stalks celery, diced
- 1 onion, diced
- 2 carrots, diced
- 3 cloves garlic, crushed, or more to taste
- 4 medium potatoes, cut into bite-size pieces
- 6–8 mushrooms, finely chopped
- 1 cup red lentils
- 3 tablespoons tomato paste
- 1 bay leaf
- 1 tablespoon smoked paprika (or sweet paprika if you prefer)
- vegan stock powder (I use Massel beef style), as per packet instructions or to taste
- ½ teaspoon chilli flakes (more if you like it a bit spicy, none if you don't)
- salt and pepper

This recipe is from my daughter, Stella Braddick. Stella starts by sautéing her onion and garlic in some olive oil. I just chuck everything into a good-sized pot with 6 cups of water – I don't use any oil.

Bring to the boil and then simmer with the lid mostly covering the pot for 25 minutes. Stir occasionally and add more boiling water along the way if it's getting too thick for your liking.

Season with salt and pepper, to taste.

Remove the bay leaf before serving.

NOTES The soupy stew keeps well in an airtight container in the fridge for 4–5 days. It also freezes well. • Always include your celery leaves for extra taste. • Be adventurous with the vegies. I often include finely chopped kale in mine. • If you want to make it even stewier, try it with a bit less water in a non-stick pot. Just make sure there's enough liquid for the lentils to absorb and vegies to cook.

SARA THOMSON

KINDNESS CASSOULET

I love to transform traditional meat-based French cuisine into vegan equivalents that are healthy, nutritious and kind. This dish is very tasty and versatile – make it your own and use your favourite vegetables.

SERVES 6

- 1 cup dried white beans, soaked overnight in cold water
- 2 carrots, diced
- 7 cloves garlic
- sprigs of parsley, leaves roughly chopped, stalks retained
- 1 sprig rosemary, leaves finely chopped, stalk retained
- 1 bay leaf
- 2 tablespoons vegetable oil
- 1 small onion or a couple of shallots, coarsely chopped
- 1 red chilli, finely chopped
- 1 parsnip, coarsely diced
- 1 swede, coarsely diced
- 1 red capsicum, coarsely diced
- 2 sprigs thyme, leaves picked
- 2 tomatoes, roughly chopped
- 1 tablespoon smoked paprika
- ¼ wombok or cabbage, sliced
- a few mushrooms, cut into quarters
- salt and pepper
- 2 thick slices rustic bread

Drain the beans and cover with fresh cold water in a saucepan. Add one of the carrots, 4 unpeeled cloves of garlic, parsley and rosemary stalks, and bay leaf. Bring to boil and simmer for 30 minutes.

While the beans are cooking, heat oil in another large saucepan. Sweat the onion and 2 crushed garlic cloves until starting to soften. Add the chilli, remaining carrot, parsnip, swede, capsicum, thyme leaves and rosemary leaves. Cook over medium heat until the vegetables start to soften (about 15 minutes). Add a splash of water if the vegies are sticking.

Add tomatoes, smoked paprika and ½ cup water, and cook for 5 minutes. Add wombok and mushrooms and stir gently. Cook for another 5 minutes. Taste and season with salt and pepper.

Preheat oven to 200°C.

Check the beans are cooked – they should be soft but not mushy. Drain, reserving a cup of the cooking liquid. Discard carrot, garlic cloves and herb stalks. Add the beans to the vegetables and stir in some of the reserved cooking liquid until the mix is very moist.

Rub the bread slices with a cut garlic clove, then chop roughly or tear into small chunks – you want coarse breadcrumbs. Mix with chopped parsley leaves and season with salt and pepper.

Pour the bean mix into an ovenproof dish or individual dishes, and top with the breadcrumb mix.

Bake in oven for about 20 minutes or until topping is crisp. It's a filling dish, so you won't need much else beyond maybe a few greens.

NOTES The bean mix will keep in an airtight container in the fridge for a week, and can be frozen for up to 3 months.

CAROL CLETHERO

NOURISHING MILLET CHILLI

This chilli dish is nourishing and satisfying, as well as being delicious. Millet is such a nutritious, high-protein grain, packed with B-complex vitamins and high in iron and magnesium as well as calcium and zinc. It's surprising how unrepresented millet seems to be in cooking generally, especially as it is very adaptable.

SERVES 4

- 1 tablespoon olive oil
- 1 large onion, chopped
- 2 cloves garlic, finely chopped
- 1 large green capsicum, chopped
- 1 stalk celery, chopped
- 1 teaspoon cumin
- 1 teaspoon chilli flakes
- ½ teaspoon ground turmeric
- 1 x 350 g jar sweet corn
- 1 x 400 g can kidney beans
- 2–3 stems silverbeet or kale, chopped
- 1 cup finely diced vegies such as cauliflower, carrot, and peas
- ½ vegetable stock cube
- 1 cup millet
- 440 g tomato passata
- 1 tablespoon tomato puree
- 1 teaspoon shiro miso (optional)
- a dash or two of tabasco sauce
- salt and pepper
- roast potatoes and a side salad or steamed green beans, to serve

Heat the olive oil in a large saucepan, then sauté the onion, garlic, capsicum and celery along with the spices until soft.

Add the sweet corn, kidney beans, silverbeet or kale, other vegetables, stock cube and 800 ml water, and bring to a low boil.

Add the cup of millet and stir briefly. Cover the saucepan and reduce the heat to simmer for 30 minutes.

Add the passata, tomato puree, shiro miso (if using) and tabasco sauce to the saucepan and stir gently. Season to taste.

Cook for another 5 minutes, then serve. It's fantastic served with roast potatoes and a side salad or steamed green beans.

NOTES Leftovers will keep in an airtight container in the fridge for about 3 days, and can be frozen. ● Leftovers can also be placed in an oven dish, covering with grated vegan cheese and baked at 180°C for about 20 minutes.

RASCALLY DOG BISCUITS

Treat your four-legged rascal with a healthy biscuit that will get their noses going! They're not only full of flavour but are high in fibre and free from sugar, oils and nuts. The sweet potato and carrot are good for digestion and are packed with vitamins, while the oats and chia seeds provide omega fatty acids to help keep your dog's skin and fur healthy.

PICTURED ON PAGE 221

MAKES ABOUT 20

- 1 large sweet potato (to give 300 g cooked), peeled and cut into chunks
- 1 tablespoon chia seeds
- 1 cup canned lentils, drained well
- 1 cup shredded carrot
- 1 cup rolled oats
- 1 tablespoon instant dried yeast
- ½ cup nutritional yeast
- 1 tablespoon parsley
- 2 teaspoons ground turmeric
- 1½ cups chickpea flour (plus more for rolling)

Preheat the oven to 200°C.

Place the sweet potato on a baking tray and roast in the oven for 30 minutes or until soft. Microwaved until soft, if preferred. Set aside to cool. Reduce oven temperature to 180°C.

Combine the chia seeds with 2½ tablespoons water. A gel will form after about 5 minutes.

In a large mixing bowl mash 300 g of the sweet potato. Add the lentils, carrot, oats and instant dried yeast. Mix well. Add the nutritional yeast, parsley, and turmeric then slowly add the chickpea flour. Add the chia seed gel and continue mixing until all ingredients are combined. Place the mixture in the fridge for a minimum of 10 minutes.

After resting in the fridge, use your hands to knead the mixture. Place the mixture on a board with some more chickpea flour and roll out to about 1 cm thick. Use a cookie cutter to make fun shapes – get creative!

Place the shapes on a baking tray lined with baking paper and cook for 15-17 minutes or until visibly browning.

NOTES Store the dog biscuits in an airtight container in the fridge for up to a week. ● Instead of cutting shapes, use your hands to roll the mixture into balls and flatten onto a baking tray to make a regular dog biscuit shape! ● The mixture makes a great filling for Kong type enrichment toys.

FEEDING GUIDE Introduce slowly if your rascal is new to treats. We recommend one to three treats per day, depending on the size of your dog.

'My life motto:
is it humane, ethical
and sustainable?'

LESLEY ECCLES

Recipe list

VANILLA CASHEW YOGHURT

TOFU FETA

BAKED ALMOND FETA

MACADAMIA CHEESE

CASHEW PARMESAN

DAIRY-FREE PARMESAN

DAIRY-FREE SOUR CREAM

CRUELTY-FREE COOKING CREAM

SOUR CREAM (CASHEW *or* TOFU)

QUICK TAHINI CHEESE SAUCE

CASHEW BECHEMAL SAUCE

HEALTHY SATAY SAUCE

GO-TO SALAD DRESSING

EASY PEANUT SAUCE

AMAZING GRAVY

MENTSUYU DRESSING

APPLE CIDER VINAIGRETTE

SIMPLE VEGIE STOCK

TOFU BACON

HOMEMADE *Basics*

Lifechanging quick recipes *that* make cooking easy

TALITHA | @THEPLANTRITIONIST

VANILLA CASHEW YOGHURT

This yoghurt brings the most dreamy creaminess to other dishes. Try it with the Chocolate Raspberry Chia Puddings on page 21.

- 200 g cashews, soaked overnight
- ½ cup oat milk
- 2 tablespoons fresh lemon juice
- 1 vanilla pod, seeds scraped
- 1 tablespoon maple syrup
- pinch of salt
- 2 probiotic powder capsules

Drain the soaked cashews and combine with ¼ cup water and all other ingredients except the probiotic powder. Blend in a high-powered food processor or blender for several minutes until smooth.

Open the capsules and add the probiotic powder to the yoghurt mix and stir to combine. Transfer to a clean glass jar with a lid and place in the fridge to set overnight.

KERYN DENROCHE

TOFU FETA

I love Greek salad and can still enjoy it as a vegan thanks to this lifechanging recipe, originally from the talented chefs at Virtuous Pie in Vancouver. My adaptation makes a good amount and keeps well in the fridge.

- 300 g firm tofu
- 140 g refined coconut oil (melted and cooled)
- 30 mls freshly squeezed lemon juice
- 1 teaspoon salt
- 1½ teaspoons onion powder

Blend all ingredients until extremely smooth. Refrigerate in an airtight container until firm, about 5 hours.

BAKED ALMOND FETA

This easy baked cheese is always a hit with my friends and family, vegan and non-vegan alike. I found this many years ago on Maple Spice, a wonderful vegan blog. Many vegan cheeses are difficult to replicate and are quite processed, so I love how wholesome and delicious this baked feta is. Do yourself a favour and make two – this cheese vanishes fast!

- 145 g ground almonds
- 60 ml lemon juice
- ½ cup water
- 3 tablespoons olive oil
- 2 cloves garlic, minced
- 1¼ teaspoons salt

Herb oil (optional)

- 2 tablespoons olive oil
- ½ tablespoon fresh herbs, chopped (I like sage, but dill, thyme or rosemary would work well)

Place all ingredients in a blender and blitz for a few minutes until super creamy and smooth. Stop and scrape down if need be.

Line a bowl with cheesecloth or muslin. A very thin, finely textured tea towel works well too.

Spoon the mixture into the cheesecloth. Bring all the sides of the cheesecloth together and tie into a ball, using a rubber band. Then place the ball in a strainer and set over a large bowl. (I attach the ball of cheese with an additional rubber band to a wooden spoon to suspend it over the bowl to help with drainage.)

Refrigerate for approximately 12 hours. This way, you can prepare the cheese in the evening and let it drain overnight to be baked the next day. After 12 hours quite a bit of liquid will have drained off.

Preheat the oven to 180°C.

Unwrap the cheese from the cloth. Transfer with smooth side up to a greased baking dish or a lined baking tray. Bake for about 40 minutes, or until slightly golden and cracked on top and firm to the touch.

FOR THE HERB OIL, heat the oil and herbs of your choice together until just warmed – don't let it simmer. Remove from heat, pour into a small bowl and leave to cool.

When ready to serve, drizzle over some herb oil over the cheese if you like. Serve with crusty French bread or toast triangles. Try it with the Crispy Crackers on page 156.

NOTES The cheese keeps for up to two weeks in the fridge – it's likely you'll eat it all well before then, though! ● I served the cheese with the herb oil the first time I made it, but haven't for the hundreds of times since, as the cheese is so good on its own.

MACADAMIA CHEESE

This basic macadamia cheese recipe can be used for any dish where you wish to add a cheesy substance into the mix. It's great for pizza. Just pop on a few tablespoons about 10 minutes before it comes out of the oven. Alternatively, you can just sprinkle some over your pizza once it's out of the oven. It takes 5 minutes to prepare.

- ½ cup raw macadamias
- ¼ cup nutritional yeast
- ½ teaspoon salt
- ½ teaspoon onion powder
- ½ teaspoon garlic powder
- 2 tablespoons lemon juice

Place all the ingredients into a blender with 2 tablespoons water and process until it has a smooth satiny texture.

NOTES Use the cheese the same day as preparing, or store any excess in the freezer. Defrost in the fridge, then loosen it up with a little water when you go to use it. ● If you're using the cheese in a dish that requires a more subtle flavour, simply substitute the lemon juice for water, so that you have 4 tablespoons of water in total. ● Blend more water through the mixture (and adjust your seasonings accordingly), and you'll have the perfect cheesy sauce. Just pour it straight over hot pasta for a quick and hearty mac and cheese.

KATIE CULPIN & JOSH BAILEY | @DELIGHTFULVEGANS

CASHEW PARMESAN

This takes about two minutes to throw together. We always have a stash in the fridge – it's so tasty, and is great on pasta, salads and toast.

- ½ cup cashews
- ¼ cup nutritional yeast
- ¼ teaspoon kala namak (black salt)
- 1 teaspoon chicken-style stock powder
- ½ teaspoon English mustard

Blend the cashews in a food processor until fine. Add the remaining ingredients and blend until well incorporated.

NOTE Store in a screw-top jar in the fridge for up to two weeks.

ERIN BATEMAN

DAIRY-FREE PARMESAN

A must-have item, my vegan parmesan has only four ingredients so it's simple and quick to make. It's perfect for sprinkling on your favourite pasta – or any dish, if you ask me!

- ¾ cup raw cashews
- ⅓ cup nutritional yeast
- ¾ teaspoon salt
- ¼teaspoon garlic powder

Blend everything in a food processor until it forms a consistent grain. Blitz the ingredients as much or as little as you like – it comes down to whether you prefer your parmesan fine or a little bit chunky.

NOTES Store in a screw-top jar in the fridge for up to two weeks. • Don't skimp on the salt – it helps to give it that 'bite' element.

EMILY COUPAR

DAIRY-FREE SOUR CREAM

I use this in any dish calling for sour cream: as a base for creamy dips, to top a baked potato, over salad leaves as a mayo substitute, and in dishes like mushroom stroganoff. It's so quick and easy! It makes about 2 cups.

- 80 g cashews
- 80 g sunflower seeds
- 1 teaspoon garlic powder
- 1 teaspoon onion powder
- 50 ml lemon juice
- ½ teaspoon sea salt

Combine cashews and sunflower seeds and soak overnight or at least 2 hours ahead of time. Drain and rinse.

Add to a food processor with remaining ingredients and 1 cup water. Blend for 1 minute, scrape down the sides and repeat until you have a smooth creamy paste.

NOTE Sour cream can be stored in an airtight container in the fridge for up to a week, or frozen for up to 3 months.

JORDAN O'CONNOR

CRUELTY-FREE COOKING CREAM

This is a super simple cooking cream substitute using just cashews and water. It's a staple in my fridge to thicken pasta sauces, soups and risottos just like the dairy version! It makes around 200 g of cashew cream.

- 1 cup cashews
- ¾ cup water

Place ingredients into a high speed blender and blend on the highest speed for around 3–5 minutes. You're after a consistency like cream where there are no granular bits of cashew left. If you want a runnier cream, add one teaspoon of water at a time.

NOTE The cooking cream will keep in a screw-top jar in the fridge for a couple of weeks.

SOUR CREAM (CASHEW or TOFU)

I do love white creamy additions to my dishes, and this recipe provides just that, but without the use of any dairy. If you're over using nuts for vegan creamy things and want something lighter, try tofu instead – it's also a more affordable way to get the same amount of satisfaction. This is marvellous with my Beautiful Beetroot Borscht (page 49). The recipe makes a little more than needed for one meal, but you can put it on anything so it won't go to waste.

- 1 cup cashews
- ½ cup rice milk, or more depending on desired consistency
- 2 tablespoons lemon juice
- 1 tablespoon apple cider vinegar, or more to taste
- 1 tablespoon savoury yeast flakes
- 1 tablespoon extra virgin olive oil
- salt and pepper, to taste

Soaked the cashews in water for at least 4 hours or better still, overnight. Drain.

Combine everything in a blender and process until creamy. Season to taste.

FOR TOFU SOUR CREAM, replace the cashews with around 150 g silken tofu. You might need less rice milk.

NOTES The sour cream keeps in an airtight container in the fridge for up to 3 days. It freezes reasonably well – after thawing, blend one more time for that nice creamy effect. • Try flavouring the sour cream with a little horseradish, or crushed garlic, or 1 teaspoon sweet paprika or 2 tablespoons chopped fresh dill.

TARNI ELDER

QUICK TAHINI CHEESE SAUCE

This is amazing on tacos, pizzas, pasta, vegies – everything!

- ¼ cup hulled tahini
- 1 tablespoon lemon juice,
- 1 teaspoon minced garlic,
- 1 tablespoon nutritional yeast
- ½ teaspoon salt

Blend with a stick blender or in a NutriBullet. Add water to desired consistency.

TARNI ELDER

CASHEW BECHEMAL SAUCE

We often toss this easy sauce through pasta as a quick macaroni cheese. It's also delicious with fried mushrooms as a pasta sauce.

- ½ cup cashews
- 1 tablespoon lemon juice
- 1 teaspoon salt
- 2 tablespoons nutritional yeast
- 1 teaspoon minced garlic

Soak cashews for at least 2 hours. Rinse. Combine with remaining ingredients and blend, gradually adding ¼ to ½ cup water until desired consistency.

HEALTHY SATAY SAUCE

I love satay sauce, but so often it's packed with additives and is very high in fat. I've been playing around with different combinations, and have finally found one that ticks all my boxes: creamy, punchy, nourishing. Yum! Add the sauce to tofu and rice bowls or vegie stir-fries, use it as a dipping sauce for roti or eat it straight from the saucepan . . .

- thumb-sized piece of ginger
- 4 cloves garlic
- 1 tablespoon vegan fish sauce (I use Red Lotus brand)
- 1 tablespoon tamari
- 3 tablespoon peanut butter (I recommend Mayver's Protein +)
- 1 teaspoon apple cider vinegar
- 1 tablespoon sambal oelek (add more or less to adjust heat)
- 100 ml plant-based milk
- juice of 1–3 limes, to taste

Peel and grate ginger and roughly chop the garlic.

Add all the ingredients to a saucepan and heat until simmering, stirring continuously. If it thickens too much, add some water. It's ready when it is the consistency you prefer.

NOTE Keeps in an airtight container in the fridge for 3 or 4 days, and can be frozen.

CHRISTINE HUTTON

GO-TO SALAD DRESSING

I use these dressing ingredients to add flavour to salads, steamed vegies and other throw-it-together dishes I make when I have nothing in the fridge or am too lazy to make something more complicated. It can rescue most dishes.

- olive oil
- tahini
- nutritional yeast flakes
- splash of tamari (optional)
- ½ teaspoon ground turmeric powder (optional)
- salt and pepper

You'll work out the balance of flavours that you prefer – be brave! Mix the ingredients together until the mixture is homogeneous. Add warm water if you want to make a thinner dressing.

JOLENE GAILITIS

EASY PEANUT SAUCE

This versatile peanut sauce is the perfect accompaniment to my Thai Fishless Cakes on page 66. It is also great warmed with a little stock and poured over roasted vegies.

- 2 tablespoons peanut butter
- 2 teaspoons curry powder
- 1 teaspoon turmeric
- 2 kaffir lime leaves, roughly chopped
- 1 tablespoon tamari
- 1 small piece ginger, peeled and chopped
- 1 tablespoon maple syrup or brown sugar

Blend all ingredients with ¾ cup water in a high-speed blender until smooth.

NOTE The sauce keeps well in a screw-top jar in the fridge for up to a week.

AMAZING GRAVY

This is the best vegan gravy recipe ever – super easy, healthy and full of flavour! I found it online courtesy of Katie Trant's Hey Nutrition Lady blog, and love how delicious it is with mashed potatoes, oven baked chips, and poured over roast vegies.

- 3 tablespoons extra virgin olive oil
- ¼ cup plain flour
- 3 tablespoons nutritional yeast
- 2 cups good quality vegetable stock, hot
- 1–2 teaspoons Vegemite
- ½ teaspoon dried thyme
- freshly cracked black pepper

Heat the olive oil in a saucepan over a medium–high heat. Once the oil is shimmering, whisk in the flour. Keep whisking for 1–2 minutes until it has a nutty aroma. Add the nutritional yeast and continue to whisk for another minute.

Add ½ cup of the hot stock and whisk into the flour mixture until it's smooth, then add the rest of the stock. Simmer the gravy for around 5 minutes, whisking constantly, until it starts to thicken and form larger bubbles.

Reduce the heat to low, and whisk in 1 teaspoon of Vegemite, the thyme and some freshly cracked black pepper.

Taste your gravy – it might need a bit more Vegemite.

When your gravy is ready, serve hot in a jug or a gravy boat.

NOTES The gravy will keep in an airtight container in the fridge for 5 days. Reheat it in the microwave or on the stovetop when you're ready to use it. ● You can also freeze it – simply thaw and reheat when you want to use it. ● Instead of Vegemite, you can use Marmite or an equivalent amount of dark soy sauce. ● Gluten-free flour can be used instead of plain flour.

MARIKA PEDRIOLI

MENTSUYU DRESSING

This versatile dressing is used in the Pokie Naddles recipe on page 36 – my take on a poke bowl.

- 100 ml soy sauce or tamari
- 70 ml mirin
- 6 x 6 cm piece kombu seaweed
- ½ teaspoon raw sugar
- dried shiitake (optional)

Combine all ingredients with 200 ml water in a saucepan and heat for 15 minutes over low heat.

NOTE The dressing will keep in a screw-top jar in the fridge for up to 3 weeks.

EMILY MORTIMER

APPLE CIDER VINAIGRETTE

This simple dressing works beautifully with leafy greens or a coleslaw. It not only costs less than a commercial dressing, it tastes better.

- ⅓ cup extra virgin olive oil
- ¼cup raw apple cider vinegar (I use Bragg's)
- 2 tablespoons lemon juice
- 1 tablespoon Dijon mustard
- 1 tablespoon maple syrup (optional)
- salt and pepper

Combine all the ingredients in a screw-top jar and shake until well combined. Taste and adjust sweetness and seasoning as required.

SIMPLE VEGIE STOCK

I love to be as sustainable as possible when I am cooking delicious plant-based meals. Therefore, I am introducing you to this nourishing 'leftovers' vegetable stock, originally inspired by Sarah Wilson. Save all your scraps throughout the week and make this over the weekend. It's loaded with nutrients, is super healthy, helps to flush out toxins from your body and boosts your immune system. Enjoy!

Vegie scraps

- carrot tops and skin
- zucchini ends
- celery bases and leaves
- potato skins
- lemon rind
- ends of turnips
- mushroom and broccoli stems
- ends of silverbeet or spinach bunches
- whatever other vegies you might have left over

Extras

- garlic, turmeric, leeks, onions, lemon juice
- any herbs you have in your fridge or garden (my favourites are thyme and sage)
- ¼ cup apple cider vinegar
- salt and pepper

Add everything to a large stockpot or saucepan.

Cover the ingredients with 8 cups of water, or fill up the pot until it's three-quarters full.

Bring to a boil, and simmer for approximately 2 hours.

Once cooked, strain the stock, season and it's ready to use or store.

NOTES This makes approximately 6 cups of vegetable stock. Use it in soups, stews or curries. • The stock will keep in airtight containers or screw-top jars in the fridge for up to a week. • Freeze it in individual cup-size portions so it's easy to use in recipes such as soups. • Replace oil with this stock when sautéing garlic or onion, or for baking your vegetables.

TOFU BACON

We love this little recipe. Hester remembers adapting it from a Buddhist chef's tempeh recipe. It's such a yummy addition to many meals – we often add it to our Mac and Cheese recipe on page 75 but it also makes a delicious addition to a vegan 'egg and bacon' sandwich or a big brekky cook-up. This makes enough for 2 to 4 people.

- 500 g firm tofu
- 1½ tablespoons olive oil
- 2 tablespoons tamari or soy sauce
- 1 tablespoon maple syrup
- 2 teaspoons liquid smoke
- 1 tablespoon nutritional yeast

Preheat the oven to 200°C. Line a baking tray with baking paper.

Cut the tofu into thin slices or small chunks, depending on what you're using your bacon for.

Mix the remaining ingredients in a small bowl and immerse tofu pieces in the mixture. You can leave it to marinate for extra flavour.

Bake the tofu for 10–15 minutes, or until it is golden and crispy on the outside.

NOTE The tofu bacon will keep in an airtight container in the fridge for up to 5 days.

KINDNESS COMMUNITY TIPS

Substitutes, hacks and secret ingredients

We asked the Kindness Community for their favourite vegan substitutes and hacks and the responses were as varied as they are ingenious. There's a ton of helpful information in the notes below the recipes and we've included the contributors' preferred products wherever they were provided.

'My best hack is simply . . . *learn to cook*.'

DEBS SAGE

TOP TEN TIPS

1. **AQUAFABA:** A fancy name for the liquid in which chickpeas or white beans have been cooked, its emulsifying and foaming properties make it a great substitute for egg whites.
2. **ASIAN GROCERS:** An absolute godsend for plant-based eaters, you'll find a huge range of tofu, tempeh and mushroom products in these stores.
3. **DAIRY:** See the homemade cheese, cream and sour cream options on pages 202–208. The community advice is to keep trying brands until you find your favourites.
4. **FISH SAUCE:** There are several vegan fish sauces on the market, for example, Red Lotus Vegan Fish Sauce and Niulife Cocomino Vegan Fysh Sauce.
5. **HONEY:** Maple syrup, rice malt syrup, agave syrup, dates and date paste are great alternatives.
6. **KALA NAMAK:** Also called Himalayan black salt, it brings great egg flavour to any dish. Don't be put off by the initial smell, your finished dish won't smell like rotten eggs.
7. **MISO PASTE:** Miso paste is an excellent magic ingredient to add to dressings and soups. Check the ingredient list – some brands contain fish products.
8. **NUTRITIONAL YEAST:** Aka 'nooch' or 'vegans' gold', this is the number one suggestion for anything that needs a cheesy taste.
9. **STOCK:** Massel products are vegan, and also free from common food allergens like gluten, lactose, artificial additives and preservatives.
10. **THE FUSSY VEGAN:** This barcode scanner app is a great help at the supermarket.

EGG SUBSTITUTES

At first, eggs present one of the biggest vegan challenges, but if you understand what you want to achieve, there are plenty of things you can use as substitutes.

Lancey Morris from @sweetlancey has one of the best summaries we've seen, so rather than reinventing the wheel, we've shared hers. Thanks, Lancey! (Try her delicious Chocolate and Sour Cream Cake on page 180.)

1 EGG =	PURPOSE	WHEN TO USE IT
1 tablespoons chia seeds + 3 tablespoons water	to bind	muffins, brownies, wholemeal and healthy baking
1 tablespoons flaxseed meal + 3 tablespoons water	to bind	muffins, brownies, wholemeal and healthy baking
½ banana, mashed	to provide moisture and sweetness	muffins, soft cookies, brownies and cakes
¼ cup fruit puree (for example, apple, pear, pumpkin)	to provide moisture and sweetness	muffins, soft cookies, brownies and cakes
3 tablespoons peanut butter	to provide creaminess and sweetness	muffins, soft cookies, brownies and cakes
3 tablespoons aquafaba	to bind and for whipping	meringues, friands, lighter cakes
¼ cup soft tofu	to add creaminess	tarts and custards
¼ cup hard tofu	to add protein and scrambled egg-like consistency	tofu scrambles, stir fries
¼ cup soy or coconut yoghurt	to provide moisture, creaminess and sweetness	muffins, cupcakes and cakes
¼ cup vegetable oil	to provide moisture	muffins, cupcakes and cakes
1 teaspoon egg replacement powder + ¼ cup water (or follow packet instructions)	to bind and provide egg-like consistency	cookies, cakes and quiches

'You really can *bake* a difference!'

PAM AHERN

'The *secret* ingredient
is the shared belief
that a *kinder world*
is not only possible,
she is on her way.'

PAM AHERN

AN EXPRESSION OF GRATITUDE

Gratitude is a noun, defined by the *Oxford Dictionary* as 'the quality of being thankful; readiness to show appreciation for and to return kindness'. And so, with this in mind, I would like to put gratitude on steroids, times it by a zillion, and flip it the way of the following damn fine human beings who have made this book possible.

To the awesome Kindness Community, who, at the drop of a kitchen pan, shared their cherished recipes of plant-based cuisine – I have been truly humbled by your generosity, overwhelmed by your creativity and my tastebuds delighted by your recipes. To all the celebrities, musicians, performers, athletes and influencers who took time out of their busy schedules and rummaged through their memories to locate and then forward their mouth-watering offerings – I welcome you to our community with open arms and thank you for spreading our message.

To the amazing Andrea McNamara, who, I think, believes in me more than I do – bless your kind heart: my world is richer for your being, and Edgar's Mission and our message of kindness so much more widely heard.

To Andrea Davison for administrative wizardry, and Hilary Reynolds for editorial detail, thank you.

To all who so deliciously brought these recipes to life: our creative design team, Nic and Pauline; our amazing photographer, Julie Renouf; stylist, Lee Blaylock; food preparers, Caroline Griffiths and Josh Nicholson; food prep assistant and baker (yummo), Emily McNamara – you cannot escape my gratitude, I love your vibrant work. I owe you all meal or two, and I promise it won't be watermelon and cucumber!

To Kyle Behrend and Kelly Dinham, who have found sanctuary and each other at Edgar's Mission – you are two of humanity's finest. Your photographs, fun and frivolity, coupled with your passion to make the world a kinder place, warms my heart no end and is deserving of far, far more than the eternal gratitude that I offer here.

To Anna Weatherlake, a stalwart of Edgar's Mission, and a lady whose kindness and passion knows no bounds – my utmost gratitude for ensuring our callout for recipes was heard by the widest audience.

To Rosemary Moore, one of humanity's finest and my friend – your ability to proofread my often jumbled writings never ceases to amaze me. I will never forget your patience and kindness.

To the team at Affirm Press, who, having already worked with Edgar's Mission on our very first cookbook, *Cooking with Kindness*, were only too willing to come back for seconds and help ensure the *Kindness Community Vegan Cookbook* was taken from the backburner of my mind, and baked to life – thank you for your energy and belief in this project.

To farmed animals everywhere, in particular the ones who will never know kindness – you forever remain the inspiration for my work, and although I may never get to know you, I love you beyond belief.

The *Kindness Community Vegan Cookbook* truly is a book made possible by the power of kindness. And so, one last expression of gratitude – to you, dear reader, for either purchasing this book, selecting it from a library shelf, or being the recipient of another's kindness. I thank you in anticipation of your contributions to making the world a kinder place by cooking and sharing in one or more of the many mouth-watering and taste-tempting recipes contained herein.

Namaste

Pam Ahern

CONTRIBUTORS

RECIPE INDEX

Wondering what to cook? We've included popular search categories below, and recommend you also check the recipe lists at the start of each chapter for a delicious overview of your options.

JACKFRUIT

KALE & SILVERBEET

LENTILS

LUNCH

MEXICAN

MUSHROOMS

NOODLES

PANCAKES

PASTA

PASTRY-BASED (SAVOURY)

PEANUT SAUCE

POTATO

PUMPKIN

RICE

RISOTTO

SALADS

SAUCES

SIDE VEGETABLES

SILVERBEET & KALE

SNACKS (SAVOURY)

SNACKS (SWEET)

SOUPS

SOUR CREAM

SWEET POTATO

TEMPEH

TOFU

ZUCCHINI

Affirm press
books that leave an impression

Published by Affirm Press in 2020
28 Thistlethwaite Street, South Melbourne, VIC 3205
www.affirmpress.com.au
10 9 8 7 6 5 4 3 2 1

NATIONAL LIBRARY OF AUSTRALIA
A catalogue record for this book is available from the National Library of Australia

Title: Kindness Community Vegan Cookbook / Edgar's Mission and Pam Ahern, authors.
ISBN: 9781922400307 (paperback)

Cover photography by Julie Renouf
Prop and food styling by Lee Blaylock
Special thanks to Made and More
madeandmore.com.au
Food preparation by Caroline Griffiths
Typesetting by Pauline Haas
Project management by Andrea McNamara

Colour separation by Splitting Image Colour Studio, Clayton, Victoria
Printed in China by C&C Offset Printing Co., Ltd.

FSC
www.fsc.org
MIX
Paper from responsible sources
FSC® C008047